Seagoing

John McCormick

Seagoing

Memoirs

Transaction Publishers
New Brunswick (U.S.A.) and London (U.K.)

Library of Congress Catalog Number: 00-021922
ISBN: 0-7658-0021-7
Printed in the United States of America

Library of Congress Cataloging-in-Publication Data

McCormick, John, 1918-
    Seagoing : memoirs / John McCormick.
        p. cm.
    Includes bibliographical references and index.
    ISBN 0-7658-0021-7 (cloth : alk. paper)
    1. McCormick, John, 1918- 2. Criticism—United States—History—
20th century. 3. Literary historians—United States—Biography. 4. Critics—United States—Biography. 5. Biography as a literary form. 6. Voyages and travels. I. Title.

PS29. M44 A3 2000
809—dc21   00-021922
    [B]   CIP

"I believe that history, properly undertaken, is the record not of what happened but of what mattered."

— Douglas Jerrold, *An Introduction to the History of England from Earliest Times to 1204*

"El pasado es pasado mientras que es presente." [The past is past even while it is present.]

— Juan Ramón Jimenez, "Es pasado"

Contents

Acknowledgments

A version of "In the Mean Time" appeared in the *Hudson Review;* "Seagoing," "The Education of an Atheist," "Brutality in Biography," and "Patriots, Expatriates, and Scoundrels" were published in the *Sewanee Review.* "In Defense of Poesie and Bullfighting," "What Ivory Tower?" [under the title, "Francis Fergusson"], and "Retiring Abroad" were published in the *American Scholar.* "Searching for Santayana" [under the title "A Most Mysterious Disaster"] appeared in the *Spectator* (London). "Brutality in Biography" also was published in *Sinn und Form* (Berlin). The portion of "Return to Berlin" concerning the June, 1953, uprising in East Berlin first appeared in *Commentary.*

I thank those journals for their hospitality to my writing.

For obvious reasons, I have often invented individuals' names in place of the originals throughout the book. I thank my former student and present editor, Laurence Mintz, for meticulous work.

My gratitude to Mairi MacInnes, my wife, for her help with this book (and everything else) knows no bounds.

Preface

The title, *Seagoing: Memoirs*, is intended to be taken both literally and symbolically, literally because going to sea was an early and desperate ambition, one fulfilled periodically in my life whether by tanker, naval warship, passenger liner, container ship, or sailboat; symbolically because I found that the many turns in a rootless life were a kind of seagoing, subject to storms, calms, hurricanes, and occasional delightful seaports at the end of long voyages. The subtitle results from a prejudice against much of what is now called autobiography, and from a conviction that the best autobiographical writing is a form of history, to which I aspire to add some small increment.

The full face of a life as usually presented to us now is rarely pretty. We have made the confessional, the scandalous, and the exhibitionistic into an exclusive form, the vulgarity of which is almost itself an art-form. To suppress nothing, to say all (excused as honesty) is to create distortion; to select is to induce form to material always unruly. Having always found the full-face, confessional treatment repugnant, I resort to "memoirs," a verbal compromise with my own history and with a hope that my adventures are somehow representative, in Emerson's sense, of my time. The Emerson of *Representative Men* rather than the Jean-Jacques Rousseau of the *Confessions* has been in my mind, if not successfully on my pages.

A central difference between autobiographers of the past (such as Edward Gibbon, Stendhal, Henry Adams, George Santayana, Graham Greene) and the often ghost-written work of notables of the present lies in the reticence of the former group. What remains in the mind after reading is event and how an event impressed the mind and being of the writer. Personality is present but not dominant; we must infer it along the way. Gibbon dwells neither on the color of his waistcoat nor on what happened to his virginity. After all, such matters are none of our business, and they distract from "what mattered," in Jerrold's phrase. I have tried to limit the personal to episodes or chapters in which for the sake of the narrative or of logic the first person indicative appeared to be indispensable.

As for the epigraph about the presentness of the past, it was fresh when Juan Ramon Jimenez wrote it, and it retained its freshness as an enduring theme in William Faulkner's fiction. Now it has become a "post-modern" cliché oddly twisted into an anti-historical device by some magic or other. I retain it for its original, fresh insight, for its ability to free us from what an Indian commentator called "the bondage of the present."

Hovingham Lodge, Scackleton
North Yorkshire, April, 1999
York, January 2000

1

In the Mean Time

Late August, 1933. My father and I stood facing each other on a street corner in St. Paul, Minnesota. I would turn fifteen in three weeks; although he was no more than fifty-two, he looked much older, frowning and troubled. "I've got ten dollars," he said, "and that's all I've got." He rummaged in his wallet. "Here's five. I'm sorry it isn't more."

"That's all right. It's plenty. I won't need much."

We shook hands and he wished me luck. "Don't forget to write," he called after me as I walked away, lugging my things in an old suitcase of his. I pretended not to hear. I wanted to get out of sight of his old once-fine suit and eternal brown hat to cover his baldness. I felt glad to be on my way, on my own, away from his gloom and silences and away from his attempt to "make a home" for me. I was on my way to the state fair grounds and a job that would pay eight dollars a week and take me out of the Depression-ridden, hateful State of Minnesota. I was free. But then I remembered that I had no address to which to write, for the good reason that my father had no address, as of that morning. I had read *The Odyssey* in school, and I thought of Telemachus trying to find his father, while I was trying to get away from mine.

In his efforts to eke out a living by selling houses, my father had met a German-born widow with a house to sell. No buyers appeared, but one day my father announced to me after school that he was going to be married to the German woman and move into her house. It was time I had a real home in place of the series of hotels and rooming houses we had lived in. I didn't like the woman from day one; she smelled of nervous sweat and Cologne water. It was obvious that she

1

didn't care for me, either. In the new household, I was required to run the vacuum cleaner, wash dishes, and go to the shops for food. In the center of her dining room table a hideous cut-glass bowl was mounted on a cut-glass pediment. While vacuuming one day, I tilted the table unintentionally, causing the bowl to totter and fall, shattering like a dropped light-bulb. The German, as I thought of her, didn't just weep, she bawled, accusing me of maliciously destroying her bowl, a wedding present from her previous marriage.

A month or so later on my way to the grocery store, I fell on the ice, and when I looked for the five-dollar bill the German had given me, it was gone. I went back to where I had fallen, but found only snow banks, the clanking snow-chains of an occasional passing car, and a sharp wind. This time the German wept the tears of rage as she accused me of stealing her money. Believing that he had resolved the dilemma my existence was to him, my father refused to see that a civil war was taking place under his nose. Occasionally there would be a truce. In one such period, I asked the German to teach me to speak her language. She was uneducated and spoke English with an accent. She was embarrassed at my request; a typical immigrant, she wanted to forget her birthplace and her mother tongue and to be a good citizen among the other German immigrants of St. Paul, Minnesota. "You should not sit reading books," she would say. "You should go out and see the city." A nervous woman, she would sit in a black or gray dress, wringing her hands and frequently adjusting her glasses.

If this is having a mother, leave me out, I thought. Before the first year of their marriage was up, separation and divorce were in the wind. I suspect that without actually lying, my father had conveyed to the German by talk of big deals in the offing, by his daily cigars and by his Californian tailored suits that he was a man of means. He in turn seemed to think that the German had been left a tidy sum by the deceased, which sum no longer existed, if it ever did have any reality. Nor can I be certain that the German actually turned my father and me out of the house, but I think she did. Toward the end, she wept continually and refused to speak to either of us. To me leaving that house was rescue from suffocation.

From my limited and selfish point of view, my father's marital disaster had one positive result. The German had a married daughter, Laura, who let rooms in her house near the fair grounds to fair people who turned up in early September, just before the annual state fair.

Laura had been kind to me; she had tried to teach me to waltz, and she provided occasional respite from the German's household. Laura treated me as an equal, an adult, and introduced me to one of her annual tenants, a Texan who traveled the country with all the apparatus of a bingo game on a ton-and-a-half truck. I begged him for a job, and he took me on, mainly to oblige Laura, I think, who was probably more to him than landlady. Whatever his motive, I was and remain grateful to him for opening layers of the world to me, the existence of which I had had no hint nor clue.

I had sat as a spectator in the theater of adult life from early childhood, and had read about it from the time I was old enough to have a library card, but now I was immersed in that longed-for state from the first hour of my new job. Hank Myers, who turned out to be the foreman of the gang of four, had arrived on the fair grounds the night before with the truck. The great tent had to be unloaded and set up, the benches and plank counters put in place, and the prizes arranged temptingly on a kind of dais above which Mr. Gray, the boss, would sit before a microphone, calling numbers drawn from a box when the whole affair was up and running. At first I called him "Mr. Gray," but later he said I was to call him Gray, as the others did. Jim, Stan, and I would sell cards to the gamblers for five cents and distribute small piles of corn grains to be placed on the numbers Gray called. The really high rollers would play two or even three cards at a time. When someone had five numbers in a row, he would shout "Bingo," and Hank would then verify the card by calling the numbers back to Gray, and the lucky winner would select a blanket or a kewpie doll or a plaster bulldog for his prize. It was all simple-minded, straightforward, and as I was soon to learn, it was honest, unlike many games at the fairs and carnivals we worked.

Our day ran from seven in the morning to midnight or later. We slept under the tent on pallets made of packaged prize blankets, covering ourselves with opened ones made of thin sleaze. Those blankets could not keep out the cold as the fall nights chilled away the summer heat. I would wash in the fair ground toilets, eat some bread and go to work dusting the benches and folding the blankets, which would serve as prizes during the day. By nine o'clock the mechanical organs on the rides would begin blaring, the ferris wheel would turn, and the farmhands would be feeding and currying the prize animals on display. At first it struck me as real, glamorous life, but in a few days the endless, repetitious noise became annoying and the early September heat made the day long. Often a farm family, man, wife, and half-grown children would stop at our tent, debating whether to invest their nickels in the chance of winning a blanket. More often than not, the man or the wife would nod no, and they would pass on to the next stall with its clicking wheel and prize hams hanging before them to be won.

"Don't let those people get away," Gray would tell us. "Call them in, sell 'em."

Hank was good at barking, the carnival term for calling 'em in. He had been working the fairs for five or six seasons and knew carny lingo. "Take the load off your feet," he would bawl. "Only a nickel for one of these gorgeous prizes," and he would gesture like a renaissance courtier at the gilded dolls. Sometimes I would try to imitate him, but I was tentative and self-conscious.

The Minnesota Fair was easier to work than briefer fairs. It went on for two weeks, so that slack times occurred when we could sit down and talk. I mostly listened to the others, who did not talk down to me, but helped me to learn how to cope with life on the road. I had only one pair of pants. Jim, a thin, tanned man of forty or so, told me to get another pair. "Why?" I asked.

"You'll get lousy, that's why. Tell Gray you have to go into town and get another pair in the Salvation Army."

Jim had been in the war and on the road ever since. He was not a professional bum, but he was a professional drunk and would work for a few weeks or months then go on a binge, riding empty boxcars between jobs. Jim, Stan, and I were paid the same wage, eight dollars a week. Hank got ten. I resolved to live on half my pay and asked Gray to hold back the other half until I asked him for it. It was Jim who convinced me that I could live on four a week: "You buy crackers and sardines when you get the chance. Don't eat fair ground food; it costs too much and it'll give you a bellyache." Sardines were ten cents a can and would make two meals on crackers. Often we had to eat fairground hot dogs or hamburgers, and Jim was right about bellyaches. I smoked a pipe and spent fifteen cents a week on a tin of Sir Walter Raleigh tobacco. The others smoked cigarettes.

The final night of a fair would always be crowded. People would have put off their visits, or plan to attend only for the fireworks which signaled the end of the fair, and also the beginning of fall. We three underlings would work the tables until midnight and after. Hank would spell Gray as caller when Gray began to get hoarse. Finally we'd drop the canvas curtains, pack the prizes, and dismantle the interior equipment. Then came the exacting job of dropping the tent, whacking loose the three-foot iron stakes with a twelve pound maul, and loading tent, prizes and all on the truck and securing the load with sisal lines. Those tasks would often take until daybreak, when Gray would set off in his small car and the rest of us would board the truck for the drive to the next fairgrounds. With luck we might have a day for setting up, but often we would set up and begin selling cards without a break.

My apprenticeship as a detached child of other people's lives proved valuable now that I had become an actor. I had grown tall fast and was badly coordinated, but watching how the others used their bodies, Hank in particular, how they stood when driving a stake and how they went about heavy lifting let me get by until the time when my coordination improved.

One evening Jim came on me in a field near the tent, where I was driving a stake, knocking it loose, then driving it again. "What in hell are you doing that for?" He stamped his cigarette in the dust.

"I'm practicing. Trying to keep my eye on the stake when I swing."

"Well, you're as green as they come, but you sure ain't yellow." From Jim that was praise, and I felt happy about it.

I liked heavy work, it made the day pass, but I was bad at it. Hank was a forebearing foreman. When I drove a tent stake too close to the tent or broke a plate on its way to the prize rack, he would only sigh, then show me how I had gone wrong. We smoked too much as we worked and broke off only to relieve thirst and other parts of the anatomy. Nobody swore, or not much, and then for considerable provocation, at what Santayana called "the authority of things." You could not force things against their implacable, unchanging nature. Hank and Jim and Stan were unskilled, but they had common sense. I learned before I was much older that the sense called "common" is anything but. Gray had common sense and dignity to go with it. A neatly put-together, small man, who with his moustache and soft Texan drawl was the very image of William Faulkner, I realized years later.

At the Iowa State Fair I became aware of two women, or girls, hanging around our tent. Both were tall and stringy, with dirty-looking long hair. They chewed gum and smoked cigarettes at the same time, flaunting their bottoms by their way of walking. I was vaguely bothered that Hank and Jim kidded around with these girls in slack times, passing them cigarettes and carrying on in what seemed to me an unmanly way. At age fifteen and three weeks I had some notion, derived from schoolyard smut and dictionary hunts, of what went on in private between married people, an idea made all too vivid by what I would come to recognize as a combination of hormones, libido, and plain lust, but my puritanical Catholic education had scarcely prepared me for the raw sexual play taking place before my eyes in the dust, the heat, and the racket from "the great midway" at that fair.

"Them's nice knees you got," Jim said to Lucille, the dark-haired, rough-skinned one. "I wonder what's up there between them?" and he laughed.

"You jest keep right on wondering, Jimmy boy." She pouted and smiled her come-on.

Like the Minnesota Fair, the Iowa Fair ran for two weeks, and the girls would show up during the empty times in the morning and sometimes in the evening as well. Occasionally in their aimlessness they would even talk to me. They taught me carny-talk, a variation of pig latin that carnival people used around laymen when they were setting up a con of one kind or another. Lucille's standard greeting was, "Heeazow's your leeaziver?" (How's your liver?) I hated it, but I was fascinated by this scurrilous secret language. The girls were not yet whores, but they were well on their way to the next station down that line.

When we finally packed up and set out in the truck for Kansas, I chided Hank, my favorite: "I can't understand what you see in those women. Chewing gum with their mouths open and smelling like dime store perfume." Hank, a natural gentleman if a rough one, merely smiled at Jim, sitting next to me, who smiled back. Neither actually answered, and I knew I was rebuked for pushing priggishly in where I had no business to be.

As we moved south, so the summer also moved with us, a good thing, too, because I had no cold weather clothing beyond a sweater, and it had turned cool and rainy toward the end of the Iowa Fair. Oklahoma was the next big one, but first we played a county fair in Missouri and a carnival somewhere in Kansas. Instead of my riding in the truck, on a long jump Gray would take me in his car to help with the driving. Eventually we would stop at a hotel, where he would stake me to a dollar room, pure luxury, for there would be a big old bathtub on lion's claws down the hall, possibly hot water, and a wonderful soak, after which I would sleep for twelve hours. I had never been South before. I had read history and fiction about the Civil War and thought of the South as an admirable land of happy liberated slaves and white warriors, noble in defeat like Robert E. Lee. The reality soon wiped out my ideal images. I did not believe that any place could be poorer than the North, but Southern poverty in the Depression, rooted in post-Civil War ruin, was bitter beyond any sweetening. Minor disaster provided my first taste of that bitterness.

We had played a carnival in Missouri but the natives seemed to go out of their way to avoid it. Gray said we would have to pull up and get out. He wasn't even "making the nut," fair jargon for meeting expenses. We had driven the truck a mile or two when it stuttered, lost power, and exuded a black cloud from the tail-pipe. Hank, driving, said "Holy smoke," and I laughed. "Shut up. Dammit, John, this is trouble."

"Pistons?" Jim asked.

"You said it."

Hank walked back to town and was gone for half a day. He had finally got through to Gray at his house in East Texas, where he had gone to tend to business before meeting us in Oklahoma City. The truck would have to be repaired in the town, and Hank was to wait for it and drive it to the Oklahoma fair grounds. Jim, Stan and I would have to make our own way there; Gray couldn't come up with bus money.

"I guess we could hop a freight," Jim said. "But they mostly go west out of here."

"Not for me," Stan said. "These southern railroad cops are bastards. They'd as soon blackjack you dead as look at you They near killed an old buddy of mine."

"Here?" Jim asked.

"North Carolina."

"It might not be so bad here. John, you never rode the rails, did you?"

"No."

"Well maybe this ain't the place for your first lesson. We better hitch-hike."

"We better get ourself cleaned up. Nobody gonna pick up a bum," Stan said.

Jim was seething, I could tell, because Gray hadn't so much as bought us bus fare, or promised to. He said he was going to take a little rest, and he might or he might not go down to Oklahoma. Stan told me to set out on the road first; one had a better chance for a ride than two, and a kid had the best chance of all. He'd follow maybe by bus if he had enough change in his pocket.

In a way I was glad to set out on my own, and I was tempted to try the boxcars that rumbled through the little towns from time to time, sometimes stopping to take on water or for some other mysterious reason. Plenty of people my age rode them, whole families rode them. You would see gaunt women with little barefoot kids, standing in the open doors of the empties as the freights rolled through crossings and towns. I wondered why so many had become so desperate, mainly farm people they appeared, but I had to put such thoughts out of mind to consider my own next move. Probably hitch-hiking was a better idea.

Not much traffic moved on the roads in that mean time, especially not in the South. I was five days covering some 400 miles, plenty of idle time between rides to see beaten-down people in wrecks of houses, dressed in near-rags and thin with the scrawniness of hunger. A few trucks went from farms to towns, and sometimes travelling salesmen in passenger cars would zoom by my begging thumb. A Negro (a polite term then) in an old Model A Ford stopped to ask where I was going. After a few miles he asked, "You got money wif you?" "I've got a dollar," I lied. I had almost three dollars. "We going to stop at this here gas station. You put a dollar of gas in the tank and we can go right on." I protested that I had to eat on that dollar.

"O.K. sonny, then you better take yoself off right here."

By contrast, I had walked five or six miles into a large town and suddenly felt nails being driven in my thigh, a cramp such as I had never had before. I had been passing the large plate-glass window of a hotel, in which a white-haired Negro bellhop had been standing. Bent over in pain out on the street, I felt myself being lifted, then supported, to hobble into the hotel, where my rescuer sat me in a large leather chair and massaged away my cramp. He refused the small change I tried to give him, saying "That's all right, that's all right." I had never experienced such kindness and have never forgotten it .

* * *

Hank Myers, Jim, and I were squatted down in the vast railway yards in Kansas City. Stan had gone to Montana, to dig potatoes, he said. I had been sick as a dog on the alkaline water at the Oklahoma Fair but had got through somehow. Jim turned up again at the Texas Fair in Dallas, still vaguely resentful, efficient, and sardonic. The Texas Fair marked the end of the season in that part of the country, and Gray had paid us off, saying he hoped to see us the next year. I collected my withholdings and felt rich, a feeling soon displaced when Gray handed me a letter from my father. He must have found Gray's home address through Laura; now he was in still one more rooming house in St. Paul and he needed money. I put five singles in an envelope with a note saying I wasn't sure of my next move. I had some satisfaction in repaying the five dollars he had given me a lifetime ago as it seemed; but my satisfaction was troubled by the fact that my capital was substantially reduced by my gesture.

We had ridden up from Dallas on a flatbed truck, but it was taking us a long time to find out where the freights were going and when. We had to dodge around two or three times a day to keep out of the way of the yard cops. It was turning cold now in November; Hank was going home to northern Iowa, and Jim hinted at female hospitality in Minneapolis. Instructed by Jim, I discarded my suitcase for a blanket roll. "You can't hop no freight with that thing in one hand," Jim said, pointing to the old case.

We weren't alone in the yard. Real bums and transients needing transport like us would meet, exchange information about freight train movements, then part and meet again. The professionals claimed to know what would move and when, but often their information was either faulty or malicious. After three days of uncertainty we decided that we would take the first empty that seemed to be going north, if only to get out of "this goddammed K.C." as Jim put it. The best bet was a train making up not far from where we were. We filled our water bottles at a stand-pipe, made up our rolls, and waited near the line for the train to begin to move. We had newspapers to wrap around our legs in the cold night.

I knew I was in for a trial. The line ran on a raised embankment of gravel, and the boxcar door would be well above that. Jim instructed me in technique: "I'll go first and open a door. Sometimes they stick. You come next, and Hank will be behind you. You have to run along that bank, throw your roll in, then heave yourself up, get it?"

At dusk, sure enough, the cars began to move, and so did we. You didn't get in when they were stopped because of the yard patrol. You knew a boxcar was empty if the door wasn't locked and sealed. Jim said "Now," and began to trot. I ran after him, ready to pitch my roll as instructed. I saw Jim heave open a partially open door as the train began to gather speed, not much, but a lot to me running in the gravel. I was almost at the door, just beyond the turning rear wheels, when I stumbled and fell. Before I hit the ground, with visions of a gory death, Hank pulled me up and said "Run, John. Get in quick." I did so, trembling, sweating and relieved beyond the telling to be alive and moving, my friends with me.

"You saved me" was all I could gasp at Hank. I felt foolish and ashamed.

"Nothing I wouldn't do for a mangy dog," Hank smiled.

"You go on tripping over your own feet, you'll end up a statistic," Jim said. Many died riding the rails in those years, one reason for the zeal of the yard police.

The train finally cleared the yards and picked up speed. Jim slid the door open a few feet and studied the cloudy sky. "I still don't know if this mother is headed north or west. Can't see no sun at all." For the first time in weeks I could sit down with nothing to do. It was luxury, even if splinters from the wooden floor worked up through my blanket. Three miserable days were behind us, and I think the others were as tired out as I was. I didn't care what direction the train was taking. As it turned out, we were heading west and had to leap out somewhere in Arkansas to beat our way back and eventually north. "No place to no where," Jim said.

There would be many trips in many boxcars over the next few years, but trips and trains fade one into another. That fading I account for not as the treacheries of memory, but because the very settings suggested the exits and entrances of characters in an excessively long play or opera. Sometimes the train would stop for no perceptible reason, and I would risk jumping down and raiding a stand of ripe field-corn, then rush back to the boxcar before it began to roll. At other stops the car would be invaded by other travelers, men looking for work or professional vagrants moving to good weather before the northern winter arrived. Some would talk, but most were glum after trying to hit me for cigarettes or makings. I was always vaguely anxious that I didn't really know where the train was going, or why. It would stop, start up again, or shunt around in the yards of some small town somewhere. When the sliding door was shut, day and night were

just about the same: boxcars had no windows. Often it was too cold
for sleep. Newspapers wrapped around the legs helped, but sometimes
they seemed to absorb the cold, not keep it out. I would get up, stretch,
light my pipe, and watch the dim bundles sleeping near me, snoring
shadows, or groaning against the swaying motion when the train got
up to speed. Sometimes the strangeness was exciting, and sometimes
it was threatening, for no reason I could put words to.

On that first journey, late one night on a siding, someone pushed
into our car, grunted, and went to sleep. In the morning he saw that I
had water in my canteen and offered me what he called "weed" in
return for a swig. I didn't know what "weed" was, but Hank defined it
for me: "Mary-Jane, marijuana. Keep away from that gink. He's a
wolf." I didn't know what "a wolf" was either. Hank said a wolf
picked up stray young kids and traveled with them. I wasn't much
enlightened, and asked why.

"They cornhole them," Jim said with disgust.

That enlightened me only dimly, but I gathered its meaning by
intuition rather than from Jim's definition. The word sounded vile and
in some dark way contributed to my growing resolve to settle in somewhere and go back to school. The theater of the boxcar soon lost any
attraction; I knew I would have to make some other kind of life for
myself. I was hungry for books again, for study, the only activity in
which I had some competence. I had fled from the German and from
my father's futilities, not from school.

Southern Iowa, and I decided I'd had enough boxcar vagaries. I
said so-long to Hank and Jim, jumped down into a deserted freight
yard, and headed for the nearby town, some groceries, and the road
north. I would hitchhike to St. Paul and go back to school, provided I
could find a night job. Two mornings later I rode into the South St.
Paul stockyards perched above an enormous, stinking hog, my com-
panion for the last several hours, the cab of the truck full of driver and
friends. I took a streetcar to Laura's, asked her to rent me a room until
I could find a job, and so rejoined the more or less conventional track.
I spent the winter heaving coal into people's furnaces first thing in the
mornings, attending school, and scrubbing pots in a restaurant on weekends. It wasn't until the end of the school year that I escaped Minnesota, although I'd still be in the Midwest. In early summer, 1934 my
aunt Gabrielle wrote me a disjointed letter urging me to come and help
her. She hadn't said why, but hinted at serious trouble. Ralph, her

husband, was out of work, and it wasn't hard to guess that they were having a bad time in that bad year, the Depression at its lowest point. This was the second time I would be going to live with Gabrielle and her husband. But even before the first time, before she was married, she had been a central presence in my life.

Before the Mean Time

Gabrielle was my mother's youngest sister. When my mother died in January, 1920, in the final sweep of the influenza epidemic that killed more people than had fallen in the World War, I was sixteen months old, and Gabrielle, then a girl of eighteen and still living at home in my grandfather's house, became my surrogate mother. Together with my French-Canadian grandfather, in theory she ruled a household that included four brothers, three of whom had recently returned from the army in France. There I remained happily until I was six years old, when Gabrielle was married and the household broken up.

My French-Canadian grandfather had emigrated from the province of Québec to central Wisconsin in about 1880, when he was twenty. His family, like his wife's, had been in Québec since the late seventeenth century without rising either to wealth and prominence, or to notoriety. Devoutly Catholic, they seem to have been artisans rather than landholders. My grandfather was a carpenter who built everything from houses to simple furniture to wooden toys for me. He never became wealthy, but he earned enough to keep his family adequately in the house he had built. Well over six feet with a rich head of gray hair and moustache, he was an imposing figure. He was uneducated, but thoughtful and analytical, an early supporter of the Progressive Party; vaguely socialist, it had been founded by Robert Lafollette, governor of Wisconsin, and aspirant to the presidency in 1924.

At age six, as the election approached, I asked him, "Grandpa, are you for Coolidge or Davis?"

"LaFol*lette*!" he laughed at me, stressing the final syllable.

Three of his four sons had gone into the army and to France between 1917 and 1919. Ernest, the eldest, had been gassed, and as a result would die in his thirties from tuberculosis. Nestor, as a French speaker, had been a runner between his infantry unit and the French; having been wounded and gassed; he would die in his early forties.

Henry was only lightly gassed, and lived into his eighties. Daniel had been too young for the war. I remember a household full of young men, and my aunt Gabrielle, all of us presided over by the magisterial figure of my grandfather. They lived frugally, as most small-town people did then, raising vegetables and preserving produce in summer for the long, cold winters, but I cannot think that they felt frugal about their lives.

Ernest was too ill to work and spent mornings coughing in bed. Having been without work for a long time, Nestor, like many who came out of the Army, finally found work in a paint shop, while Henry sometimes had part-time work in a soft drink bottling plant. Before he enlisted, Dan, something of a rakehell, would roar about on what my grandfather called "That got-tamn motorcycle." Beset by housekeeping, for which she had little talent, Gabrielle ("Gaby" to me) was often teased by her brothers. They teased her when she had her hair bobbed, and when they came on her dancing slowly to my favorite record on the wind-up gramophone, "The Letter Edged in Black," and on the reverse, "The Prisoner's Song." She and her brothers horsed around a lot, once breaking a large window in the front door, which they frantically tried to replace before my grandfather returned from his carpenter's shop in town. They feared his explosive *"Encanaillement! "* which he would shout when things got out of hand in the house. Gabrielle would maneuver a button-hook on my shoes and walk me with her to the public library. She would take out novels, and for me the children's books which my grandfather would read to me in his heavy French accent. When we were alone he would always speak to me in French, and on Saturdays, lured by the cliff-hanging serials, we would walk downtown to the picture show at the Ideal, where he would roar with laughter at Charlie Chaplin, Harold Lloyd or Buster Keaton. I did not find Chaplin funny, but I liked the others, especially the westerns with Hoot Gibson or Tom Mix.

I cannot recall a harsh word or a slap. When the circus came to town, Ernest arranged for me to have a ride on the elephant's head, and in summer when the ice man approached in his dripping wagon, I was allowed to run down the block to be hoisted on the horse's back for the ride home. In the early spring, the men would dig a large vegetable garden, which my grandfather would tend. In the fall he would put down carrots and potatoes in the sand floor of the basement. In spring, his breakfast was radishes and bread which he baked himself, and in winter he would make a tub of pea soup seasoned by a large hunk of smoked ham, put it on the back porch to freeze, and chop it off as needed with a hatchet. He made soap for washing clothes from kitchen-grease and lye.

Grumblings and arguments erupted in the household, but they swept over me for the most part. I learned misery when Nestor brought me a collie pup and someone poisoned it within a week. Bodily miseries were treated with home remedies: a stick of clove for toothache; a purge for bellyache. No doctor was ever called, no dentist visited. Teeth were brushed with salt or baking soda. I was seen to by Gaby, to whom I must have been a burden. She was a spirited and pretty girl with black hair and brown eyes. She must have longed for time with her friends, but the household occupied her fully. For recreation, the house offered an upright piano, which she played inexpertly, two novels by Rafael Sabatini, and the Victrola. As the only child in the place, more or less cosseted, I must have been spoiled, but how is the spoiled child to know he is spoiled? Eventually I realized that people were kind because they thought I suffered for lack of a mother, but I had no such feeling, then or later.

All good things come to an end. After kindergarten and first grade in the Catholic school, Aunt Gabrielle told me that she was going to be married and move away, and that Grandfather was to go and live in Florida with my Aunt Hélène. Her brothers had drifted off to jobs and marriages. My father, in Detroit now, had sent for me. With two dollar bills pinned to my underwear I was put on the train for Chicago, where my father would meet me in the central station, and together we would go on to Detroit.

On the train, the conductor talked to me and brought me drinks of water in fragile triangles of waxed paper, and in the station at Chicago he took me into the waiting room and sat me down on a bench, which looked like the pews in church, before returning to his duties. It seemed a long time before I saw my father approaching, and when he drew near, I pretended not to recognize him. I knew he was hurt, but when he tried to kiss me I turned my head. At once I was ashamed, but I didn't know how to tell him. So began more than a year of life in a hotel room with my father, to be followed by three years in Illinois with my aunt Gabrielle and her husband, Ralph Martin.

Waukegan lay on a bluff above Lake Michigan. The lake-front was given over to coal docks, an asbestos plant, and other industrial chaos, except for a stretch of sandy beach offering some relief from the frying heat in summer. Up the hill from the beach were the Victorian gingerbread houses of the solid citizens, and a mile away, in what had been empty fields, streets of new, identical bungalows, built by a speculator in the few good years between 1925 and 1929–30.

My uncle by marriage, a short, neat, physically tough man, had left his home in upstate New York to join the cavalry (always pronounced "calvary") and had ridden under Pershing into Mexico to pursue Pancho Villa in 1915, an episode which reflected glory even on me, I thought, just as my real uncles' wartime service set me apart from other boys. Uncle Ralph bore severe facial scars from a man-hole fire in New Orleans, where he worked for the telephone company. Intelligent but inarticulate, he had set out through marriage and fatherhood to settle down after years of wandering. He had taken instruction and become a Catholic in order to marry my aunt, and was more fervent than she in observing the sacraments. He earned reasonable wages as a telephone cable repairman in Waukegan. With a heavy mortgage, he had bought one of the speculator's bungalows and furnished it on small weekly payments to a collector who appeared every Friday.

My father had contracted to pay the Martins for my upkeep, but all too soon letters from Los Angeles, where he had gone to make his fortune, failed to arrive. Without a word on the subject having been spoken, I realized my actual position in the household. Despite their reticence, I knew that I was a burden and should try more than before to help about the place. Vaguely I felt shame on behalf of my father, and slowly I came to resent his silence. The time in Waukegan was otherwise tolerable, although at Christmas something occurred to call in question my automatic, unthinking reliance on Gaby. One of my father's sisters, my aunt Jen whom I had never met, sent me a golden fountain pen, a beautiful object and a flattering one, an adult appurtenance rather than a child's toy. I longed to grow up, and my fountain pen was a token of a golden, adult future. By the new year, however, my fountain pen had disappeared. I treasured it too intensely to have lost it, and I asked Gaby if she had seen it.

"I borrowed it. It's too good for you to take to school. Someone might steal it. I'll keep it safe for you with my things."

I couldn't answer her treachery, which made me miserable to the point of tears. Even my father would not have done such a thing. A refuge had been snatched away; in the future I would have to be wary.

I made friends with children in the neighborhood and learned to play baseball and football. My uncle Ralph set up a workshop in his basement, where he taught me to use tools and the mechanics of small electrical motors. He let me work with him as he tore down the motor of his old Essex, a four-wheeled disaster from the day it left the factory and came third-hand to him. He would slip me a quarter now and then, and I would mow lawns for other quarters. The nuns in school were good to me and encouraged me to read in the public library; the school "library" consisted of some twenty-five grubby volumes. The nuns also urged all of us boys, unsubtly, toward the priesthood: I was assured that one day I could be a bishop. Whatever my ambitions for the future, the priesthood, much less a bishopric, formed no part of it. Suddenly I had found certain girls sinfully enthralling.

As a second child was born to the Martins, I felt increasingly isolated from their family circle, though not by their design. Money was short, as were the Martins' tempers. Clothes were a worry, for I was growing fast and winters were as fierce on that lake shore as the summers were hot. Occasionally I would surprise my aunt alone and weeping in a chair; otherwise it was a good episode in my young life. I was not at all happy to rejoin my father when again he returned to Detroit, where, on salary for a change, he wanted to try to look after me. The year was 1929, and his salary soon became as illusory as the prosperity of the country at large.

* * *

Arriving back in Waukegan in late June, 1934, I found matters changed in the Martin household. As I came to the door at midday, I found my aunt in a passion with a grubby man in a shiny suit, who soon left saying, or threatening, that he'd be back. "It's the collector, I'm sick of him and now he claims he's going to re-possess my sewing machine—I'm glad you came, John," tearily, all in one breath, and she kissed me. "How am I supposed to make clothes for these children, and no sewing machine?" She spoke more quietly, as though to herself. "How tall you are. You're going to look like your mother," she added apropos of nothing.

The house, formerly as neat as young children permitted, was no longer so. A musty smell emanated from a basketful of damp and moldy laundry, and the door knobs were sticky with some substance— jam? An infant, my aunt's third child, lay mewling in his crib. Gaby had changed too. Once slim and petite, now she was fat, and her summer house-dress was far from clean. She picked up the baby and prepared for the indelicate business of changing its diaper.

"I wrote to you because I didn't know what else to do," she explained. "It's Ralph. He's drinking up everything we have and there's almost no work." The words poured out in a rush. She got up with the child and made for the kitchen. "Look at this, just look." She pointed at the ceiling, stippled irregularly in green-gray, moldy patches. "It's his beer. He bottles it and drinks it too soon. Then when he opens it, it explodes." I wanted to laugh, imagining that bottle drama, but Gaby's distress was intense and immediate. She had her brothers to turn to for help but they could do little for her; they had their own troubles. My grandfather sent a few dollars from time to time, and Dan had sent fifteen dollars. Mr. Moody at the grocery gave her a little credit, but he needed to be paid too. "Nothing in Papa's house back home ever prepared me for this. If you could just help me around the house, the way you used to. And try to talk to Ralph, he always liked you and maybe he'll listen to you. He won't listen to me." According to Gaby, Ralph had changed from a sweet-tempered husband and loving father into a careless brute who ignored his children and accused her of getting fat and lazy. All he did was drink his damned beer and complain. The bank was letting them stay on even though they hadn't paid the mortgage for months. They could be turned out at any time.

It was flattering that in my sixteenth year Gaby thought I could influence Ralph, a man in his forties, and a former "calvaryman" at that. By the end of the week, however, I began to feel trapped and resentful. The two older children zipped around the house out of control, shooting me, Gaby, the mailman, and passing dogs with cap-guns. Gaby slopped about the house, accomplishing little. I remembered my grandfather's *"Encanaillement!"* I wanted to go back on the road to try and find a summer job, but Gaby's dilemma prevented a move even as it added to my resentment.

The Martins' downfall took on another face when I talked to Edith next door, the Swedish neighbor who had been a special friend and refuge in my childhood. "I told Gabe years ago never to lose her credit," Edith said. "Instead of keeping up her payments when Ralph was making good wages, Gabe would go out and buy things they couldn't afford. Now it's too late, and she just lets herself go. You can't blame it all on Ralph." Edith told me how Ralph's work had faded away as the Depression took hold. First there was no more overtime at time-and-a-half pay, essential to their budget. Then he was on half-time, which was bad enough, but by 1932 they called him out only after a storm or some such emergency, and no one could bank on storms. He had always made home-brew in ten-gallon crocks next to the furnace, like many people before repeal of the Volstead Act. Ralph kept on making it after repeal; it was cheaper to buy yeast and hops in a large can from Mooney's store than the official product of the breweries. At first he would drink more than one bottle only on weekends, but as work dwindled and bills accumulated, his intake equalled, then began to exceed his production. Hence the messes on the kitchen ceiling above the work table.

One beery evening, Ralph gave me his version of events. He had done his best to keep things together. He had pleaded with his foreman to be kept on, but the company was letting maintenance go to hell anyway, and there was no work, even for men more senior than Ralph. Gabe had complained when he took money to pay installments on an electrician's qualification course, and complained when he bought tools. She had began to let herself go and neglected the children. He it was who bathed them and put them to bed and told them stories. Gabe thought jobs were out there on trees, but there weren't any jobs. The big asbestos plant had closed down except for the guards. Everyone they knew was out of work, and even people like Scanlon down the block, who had his own garage, he was going to throw in the towel and go West.

Ralph was not exaggerating. After two weeks I got a job in the big hotel cleaning vegetables and washing dishes. It was over 100 degrees in the kitchen and I hated it, but however resentfully, I was able to pay Gaby a few dollars and so help keep things turning, however crankily, in their house. About the time I had to leave to go back to school in St. Paul, Ralph disappeared one night just after Labor Day and never came back.

Years later his daughter Jeanne wrote to me from Florida asking what her father was like, and had I ever any trace of him? I wrote back that he was a fine man pushed beyond his limit; I told her how he had taught me years before down in the basement, and how content he seemed then, in his own place and with his own family, after his aimless early years.

One of my Wisconsin aunts looked after Gaby's two older children for the next many months, while she stayed with Edith. A year later she moved in with non-drinking, non-smoking fundamentalist carpenter, and eventually married him.

My aunt's history was not isolated, nor was mine. People were simply perforated by the Depression called Great. Some survived and were fortified by the experience; others like my father, lapsed into bitterness, or like Ralph Martin, vanished without trace. History icily recounts what happened; what matters lies in our memory of the long, long haul.

2

Origins:
The Education of an Atheist

Having been to sea as scullion and deck-hand, upon joining the Navy when World War II began, I had thoughts of becoming an officer and a gentleman. In the recruiting office, the first form I was to fill in asked my religion. I pencilled in "atheist," even though I had not fully thought through my position with respect to God or the gods: I was to agree with the novelist Dermot Healy, one of whose characters, an Irish language tutor, says, "I love the man who made the world, but I don't believe in him." The chief petty officer in charge, who looked like an alcoholic bishop, inspected my form and told me, "Son, I wouldn't put that down if I was you." The Navy didn't like atheists. It was going to be a long war, and I might want to be promoted. He erased "atheist" and carefully printed in "Prot.," so an official "Prot." I remained for the duration.

To one of my upbringing, to be described as a Protestant was little different from being damned to hell as an atheist. My parents and their forefathers, French and Irish alike, had always been Catholics, hence I had been baptized and brought up in accordance with the Jansenist-like form of Catholicism current in the Midwest of the 1920s. My early residence in my grandfather's house did nothing to challenge my cradle Catholicism.

Grandfather was devout as a matter of course, observing all the prescribed rituals, but he was hardly a Jansenist. Among my earliest memories I see the parish priest playing poker with Grandpapa and my uncles, sipping the bootleg whisky that he had brought, as he glanced at his hole-card. Before World War I an aunt of mine had married Louis Leclair, a French-Canadian saloonkeeper in the town. When prohibition arrived in 1919, he continued to keep his saloon, now with a partner, and for this breach in the law, one of the partners would go to the county jail for thirty days. They took turns, following the semi-annual raid, always signaled by an apologetic warning from the sheriff, who had gone through the eight grades at St. Anthony's with Louis and had served with him in Cuba in the Spanish-American War.

In the first grade myself at St. Anthony's, I recall a nun supervising us children as we walked in line from school to church and commanding us to walk straight: only Protestants shambled as we were doing. Each day we had half an hour of religious instruction. We began to learn by rote the Baltimore Catechism, and once a week the poker-playing priest would ask us to recite it, while explaining the meanings of hard words. If a child came to school with a dirty neck or black fingernails, Sister Cecilia would send him home with a note to his parents. Later, in other Catholic schools in other towns, dirty fingernails meant a whack on the knuckles with a ruler.

Religious instruction, indoctrination rather, became increasingly intense through the eight grades. In the first three grades we were taught the Palmer Method of penmanship (which I failed), reading, arithmetic, and a form of history and geography imparted by way of lives of the saints, stories of martyrs, and homilies deriving mainly from the New Testament. Often I had nightmares about missionaries flayed and roasted alive by the pagan Iroquois. We were discouraged from actually reading the Bible, even the Douay version. When we asked why, Sister Dorothea told us that parts of the Bible were unsuitable for Catholic children. Inevitably that sent several of us hunting for Bibles in order to find the unsuitable parts. The concepts of adultery and coveting another man's wife stopped us for a time. Words such as "fornication" sent me to the dictionary, which I soon found to be a prolific source of other words a child would hear and know by instinct to be licentious and probably sinful.

Sin occupied a major part of our indoctrination and of my waking life. If we could not be lured into faith by stories of miracles and roasted Jesuits, then we surely could be frightened into virtue by the nuns' accounts of Limbo, Purgatory, and Hell. More often than not in Sunday sermons, the priests would dwell on the sufferings of the damned in terms that, I later decided, made James Joyce's account of

Stephen Dedalus's indoctrination look like Peter Pan. I could accept that if I murdered someone it was only just that I should go to hell, if I had the bad luck to die unconfessed. I had much greater trouble with the assurance that I had a guardian angel who would try to protect me from murder or other sins. Even in the second grade the idea of a guardian angel, always present, never asleep, struck me as preposterous, and something like an intrusion. I was not alone in that. My schoolmates and I wondered whether angels urinate and defecate; I thought not, but others thought otherwise. Sister Caroline went red in the face when I questioned her about the existence of guardian angels and accused me of showing off. Her impatience was an exception; in the main the nuns were kind to us all; they were extraordinary women and quite beautiful in their wimples and flowing black garments. "Reformed" into modern garb, their loss of dignity and authority seems to me to border on the tragic.

At age eight I was nominated to the parish priest as a potential altar boy, and given extra instruction in the responses of the Latin mass. Since formal Latin began only in the fifth grade, I parroted the responses without the slightest idea of their literal meaning. That did not bother me, for most of what we did and heard was ritualistic and mysterious. All Catholics were set apart, chosen and fortunate, and altar boys were particularly chosen. It gave life added meaning to get up at five A.M., walk to the church in all weathers, don a black cassock and white starched surplice, then light the candles on the altar and prepare the tray of wine and water for the Consecration. We altar boys competed to serve at weddings and funerals, after which the priest or the families would reward us with a quarter or half dollar.

The Church considered seven the age at which a child could distinguish right from wrong: we were then ready for the sacraments of Confession and Communion. Long hours went into the distinction between venial and mortal sin. Was saying "damn" a sin? Yes, a venial sin. Was "goddamn" a mortal sin? Evasion: it hurt God to hear that, and good Catholics never wanted to hurt God. That did not square with experience. My Catholic relatives often goddamned somebody or something in apparent spiritual serenity, but I kept my peace. When the great day of our first Confession finally arrived, my friends and I were worried. Some hadn't committed any sins they knew about; I had no trouble here, for I cursed regularly and lost my temper with ease. After our trips to the sinister enclosure of the confessional, we got together to find out what penance the priest had exacted. I felt let down to learn that each of us, boys and girls alike, had merited three Our Fathers and three Hail Marys, plus the obligatory Act of Contrition. By age ten, I was getting five Our Fathers and five Hail Marys, progress of a kind. When I turned twelve, the priest listened to my accounts of swearing and raging, then began to ask questions that made me squirm. Did I have impure thoughts or commit impure acts? I certainly had plenty of impure thoughts, carloads, but I wasn't sure what he meant by impure acts. Like my guardian angel, if any, I thought my confessor was intruding in an unjustified way. I would keep my thoughts to myself.

First Communion, as opposed to Confession, was not only untroubling but a joy. Now I experienced for the only time in life the transcendent, what I was to learn from Rudolf Otto's *The Idea of the Holy*[1] to call the numinous, that aspect of deity that defies comprehension in rational or merely ethical concepts. Where miracles, guardian angels, sin and punishment had created hurdles of semi-belief, transubstantiation offered no difficulty, my first (and last) experience of *credo quia impossibilis est*. Of course the priest's quaffing of wine was the blood of Christ, and without question the wafer melting in my mouth was His mystical body. I floated away from the communion rail knowing that the mystery of grace existed and that I was in that state. My nascent skepticism was gone. It was soon to return, but for a month or two I was a pushover for whatever the priest and nuns served up as dogma.

As memory of that first ineffable communion faded over months, then years, it was replaced by the continual and often successful efforts of priests for the boys, nuns for the girls, to terrify us with oblique accounts of what sexual acts, conveyed through lurid hints never specified, could do to body and soul. What exactly took place in sexual activity we never learned from the Church; my own instruction came from schoolyard smut, inference from adults' badinage, and from reading. During one Holy Week, an itinerant Benedictine specializing in holy smut for the pubescent was invited to our school to describe the various venereal diseases that we would surely contract from evil

---

1. Rudolf Otto, *The Idea of the Holy: An Inquiry into the Non-rational Factor in the Idea of the Divine and its Relation to the Rational*. Tr. John Harvey (Oxford: Oxford University Press), p. 31.

thoughts or sinful women. That B-grade Savonarola glared at us as though we were already lost, saliva flying from the pulpit as he raved on. Finally he would change key: married love awaited us, perhaps, when we were grown men and women; meanwhile whenever evil thoughts crept upon us, inspired by Satan, prayers to our patron saint and to the Virgin Mary would defeat Satan and keep us chaste for our virginal mates in some impossibly vague future.

How often we were assured that worldliness would lead us to the quicksands of sin; the flesh was vile; the Devil lurked just around each moral corner: these were the precepts which the Catholic Church gave us to protect us from the world, in which for better or worse, most of us would have to make our way. The only genuine protection for a boy was to become a priest, and for girls, the nunnery. By age thirteen I could imagine keeping the vow of Poverty; Obedience would be hard but possible; but as for Chastity, the prospect of an entire celibate life was horrible. I counted the long years before I should be old enough to marry a voluptuous, virginal woman. Active apostasy began in that fraught region, aided by increasing skepticism. The years of scratching a living in the Depression did little to validate the moral precepts of a Catholic education. It would take many years for those precepts to lose their power, for I believe that I was not irreligious by nature, but experience made my equipment for what people call "the real world" seem inadequate if not iniquitous.

At age eighteen I came back from a stint at sea to attend mass in the cathedral at St. Paul, Minnesota. There I heard that Catholics were instructed to pray for the success of General Franco's uprising in Spain. Normally the Church sided with established governments, the pastoral letter informed us, but we were to understand that the established government in Madrid was composed of atheistic red communists who must be defeated. I found this outrageous stupidity: it violated everything I had known first-hand in two voyages to Spain, and everything I had read about recent Spanish history. I never again entered a Catholic church as a communicant.

Time and again I had gone to priests with my doubts, political and religious. I had read everything I could lay hands on about the nature of belief, including Pascal and his famous wager. The only priestly response I ever got was, "Have faith, my boy, and pray for God's guidance." That answer was not so much a reflection on Catholic teaching as on the intellectual quality of the priesthood in the Midwest as I encountered it. Those priests were well-fed, purple-nosed, lazy, and ignorant. I was fifteen years older and far gone in agnosticism before I met, aboard the *Île de France,* a well-educated, eloquent, casuistical Jesuit. He was so open-minded that he seemed heretical; had I met him and his fellows at a younger age, I might well have remained in the church far longer. People who would reform Catholicism often complain of "a right-wing authoritarian element" in the Church. This strikes me as naïve, for one of the sources of strength in the Church in the past was that by definition it was authoritative (not authoritarian), while in the United States and most other countries, it has always been right-wing, intolerant of worker-priests or the intellectual maundering of converts such as Simone Weil in France or Allen Tate in Tennessee, USA.

I did not leave the Church without a pang. Although my early education had been a kind of psychological boot camp, I continued to find the Latin mass beautiful; some of the hymns we sang in our endless church-going stay with me sixty-five years on, and the various rituals of the ecclesiastical year gave meaning and solidity to my rootless existence, just as being a Catholic had given us school children a distinct identity, making us feel somehow special, even saved, if we watched our step.

I had spent my early years among people who took religious faith for granted, who observed the tenets of Catholicism more or less strictly, and who derived great comfort from their faith in the bleak years of deprivation and unemployment. I came to envy them their faith. It gave them steadiness, it made them fairly good citizens, and it prevented the existential despair that was to become fashionable in circles I later frequented. Work in fairgrounds, mills, factories, restaurants, and hotels meant rubbing shoulders with Protestants, many of whom were as solid and unthinking in their religions as the Catholics of my boyhood. Others were indifferent, never having given thought to moral questions of any sort. I became less of a Catholic prig, gradually, and found myself turning (in my mind) to "Cigarettes, Whisky and Wild Wild Women," while reality offered pipe tobacco, beer, and shy studious girls. By the time I entered university, the girls were less shy, but still studious. I made friends with ideological atheists among people studying philosophy, several of whom were Trotskyites, Stalinists, or socialists of one stripe or another. They all contributed to my inevitable break from any vestige of religious faith; their arguments had a comforting, bull-session validity that produced for me a rare sense of solidarity. I attended meetings of the various radical groups, each of which wanted to sign me up. The party organizers, fresh from New York City or from Trotsky's bodyguard in Mexico, were ardent to the point of fanaticism, reminding me of the missionary priests of my childhood. When war came, the Trotskyites expounded, we were to join up and learn to use weapons so that we could turn them on the capitalist oppressors when peace returned. Their humorless expounding of Marx, Lenin, Trotsky, and Stalin made little sense to me: the working class, which, unlike most of the expounders, I had actually worked in, was not about to rise up and take over. Also I could not sing the songs with a straight face, those of the Spanish Civil War excepted. Religious faith and revolutionary fervor lay in the same basket; the triumph of the working class was as unlikely as the triumph of the soul in heaven or its eternal sufferings in hell.

The outbreak of the World War II in 1939 was an enormous event for all of us: vast changes both threatened and invited us. Born during the first war, brought up on war stories, acutely aware of Manchuria, Ethiopia, and Spain, we knew in our bones that our war was on its way. Some of us wanted to go to Canada to enlist, but we were advised to complete our university degrees: we would be of greater use as officers than as enlisted men. August 1939 brought the Hitler-Stalin pact and the end of our chilly flirtation with Stalinism. A few true believers remained loyal, finding Byzantine reasons for Stalin's treachery, but most of my immediate group happily kissed goodbye to that ideology. Religious faith, politically radical faith, patriotic faith, that new religion, each offended in its way. War meant the suspension of reason, variously valid appeals to nationalistic unreason, and, as I discovered on active service, occasionally the union of religious and patriotic faith.

The wartime cliché that there were "no atheists in foxholes" I came to see as egregious propaganda. Although no one could dig a foxhole aboard ship, the messiness and suppressed panic of action produced plenty of blasphemy but no detectable prayer, no detectable enhanced holiness among either the believers or the indifferent. Some of the quality of the experience appears in Büchner's *Dantons Tod*, in which Danton, imprisoned and awaiting the guillotine, remarks, "Why do I suffer? There's my rock of atheism." As for me, had I believed in God I would have cursed Him for the war and the excrescences that came to public knowledge during and after it. Faith turns to hatred when the killing begins, as the religious wars of the past, and of the urgent present, testify. Killing without ideology turns some men into indifferent brutes, but not into believers in an omniscient God whose fathomless mystery in permitting wars must be accepted as a test of faith. Where now was Rudolf Otto's *"mysterium tremendum "* which could move from sublime feelings to "wild and demonic forms and can sink to an almost grizzly horror and shuddering?"[2] This attempt to account for divine savagery was consistent with Otto's belief that "there are two equally dangerous extremes: to shut reason out, and to let nothing else in," but to me equally unsatisfactory. I suspect that the foxhole created atheists out of believers and rarely transformed the peacetime skeptic into a believer.

"To shut reason out and to let nothing else in" requires the pretrance disciplines of the mystic, self-hypnosis, or drugs, none of which is attractive to the skeptic. Mysticism means the abandonment of objectivity, of irony, humor, of civilized discourse, qualities that make existence bearable and sometimes enjoyable. At the other extreme, the ardor of atheists often turns into a fanaticism not distant in quality from the religious faith of the mystic or the fury of the political fascist. Often the atheist's arguments abandon objectivity and irony, added to which pompousness and abuse occur in place of the sublime prose and splendid poetry of some mystics. There was a lot to get through if I was going to order my semi-beliefs and prejudices, for my thoughts were like migrating birds blown out of formation by heavy winds. The route was as long as it is familiar. It began with Lucretius, on to Plato, to Tertullian's obscurantism, which I loathed. When Herbert Feigl, a refugee and one of the founders of the Vienna Circle of logical positivists arrived at the University of Minnesota in my senior year, I began to see a less emotional basis for an evolving position. Feigl told us that the statement "God exists" is not a logical proposition. That chilly but convincing view was upheld for me by the lady who said that to debate the existence or nonexistence of God is like eating soup with a fork.

My undergraduate friends and I had flippantly taken either agnosticism or atheism for granted. Unbelief had been a conviction, to be sure, but it was also a fashion, and I had taken comfort in conformity

---

2. Rudolf Otto, *The Idea of the Holy,* pp. 12–24.

to nonconformity. Feigl's positivism disabused us of flippancy and introduced me to the painful process of thinking with as small a ration as possible of emotion. The war brought a long hiatus to undergraduate luxuries like logical positivism. As a graduate student after the war, I tried to get back to where I had left off (an impossibility in itself). The war had done nothing to challenge my thoughts about religion, and readings in Anselm and Aquinas amounted to the same effect as the war. The ontological proof of God's existence, or the notion of "disembodied consciousness," seemed no more than a jargon or mechanism having nothing to do with faith, or belief. I hung on to Hume, with his motto, "Keep sober and remember to be sceptical," and to his words on miracles in *An Enquiry Concerning Human Understanding*, "no testimony is sufficient to establish a miracle, unless the testimony be of such a kind that its falsehood would be more miraculous than the fact, which it endeavours to establish." For Hume, the defect in Christianity is that it was established on miracles "and even to this day cannot be believed without one." Gibbon's scathing treatment of miracles, even as he thought to establish rational grounds for them, I found amusing in their illogicality. Diderot and Deism, that evasion of atheism; Shelley, Schopenhauer,[3] even Nietzsche, although I distrusted him, all added to the salad of my atheism. Although I wanted to think that I was being Feigl-like in my approach, I knew very well that I was more moved by the literary style of the writers I admired than by thought abstracted from style. I could never be a Feigl.

I had read the English mystical poets: Quarles, Herbert, Crashaw, as an undergraduate and read them with pleasure. Later, when I knew Spanish, I read St. John of the Cross and Santa Teresa of Avila with equal pleasure. Their mysticism seemed far removed from and superior to the struggle of theologians to convince people in purportedly logical argument of the being and qualities of God. The mystics' conviction of faith took its power from superb poetry; they did not set out to challenge the skeptic nor to convert the nonbeliever. Their work enhanced the psychological attraction of religion, just as Latin hymns,

---

3. Schopenhauer's definition of conscience: "one-fifth fear of men, one-fifth fear of the gods, one-fifth prejudice, one-fifth vanity and one-fifth habit." Quoted in Iris Murdoch, *Metaphysics as a Guide to Morals* (London: Chatto & Windus, 1992), p. 251.

Romanesque churches, and the great cathedrals did. I was struck by the *relative* absence of religion in the most enduring literature in English in the eighteenth and nineteenth centuries. William Blake invented his own God and his own theology. Religiosity rather than religion was apparent in Wordsworth, Matthew Arnold, Tennyson, and George Eliot; an occasional vicar in Jane Austen's novels does not constitute religion, but only a comment on social gradations in the period. Apart from Gerard Manley Hopkins in the nineteenth century and Graham Greene in the twentieth, I found it difficult to think of first-rate religious work in modern imaginative literature. I came to believe that the priests, on the other hand, the Protestant clergy, the rabbis and the mullahs were each in varying degrees trying to implant and to maintain an ideology, and ideology, whether benevolent or malevolent, was the ultimate enemy. At the same time there was no question that the classical atheists, too, were advocating an ideology.

Holbach, the first and the loudest of the fire-snorting atheists, extended the field of attack from theology to civics. In one of thirty pamphlets he published between 1760 and 1770, he wrote that the immoral oppose religion because it censures them, and others despise it as ridiculous, and still others are indifferent only because they are unaware of its true disadvantages. "But it is as a citizen that I attack it, because it seems to me harmful to the happiness of the state, hostile to the march of the mind of man, and contrary to sound morality, from which the interests of state policy can never be separated." Holbach saw no point in the argument that religion helped to keep the vulgar multitude in order. "Do we see that this religion preserves them from intemperance, drunkenness, brutality, violence, fraud, and every kind of excess?" In Holbach I thought I heard the authentic tones of the ideologist, also to be heard in differing keys in Shelley, Feuerbach, Comte, Marx, Nietzsche, Lenin, Stalin, and their progeny. Nietzsche's literary power, which had interested me mightily as an undergraduate, seemed to place him in a category different from most of the others. When I re-read him years later, he seemed shrill and indeed on the way to the madness that finally overwhelmed him.

I groaned when I found Thomas Huxley's work on a required reading list, but I soon came round to appreciate him as the St. Paul to Darwin's evolutionary hypothesis. He spoke with a natural scientist's authority against "the cruelty, the lies, the slaughter, the violation of every obligation to humanity" of Christianity. His passion, unlike

Nietzsche's, was not shrill; his tone was witty and urbane. I think that Huxley's writings mark an intellectual division between metaphysical arguments about religion that for centuries had dominated discourse, and the efforts of later churchmen to accommodate God and religion to the hypotheses and facts of natural science and later forms of logic. Bertrand Russell's many works on ethics and religion would seem to owe a great deal to Huxley.

Russell, too, was nothing if not urbane, witty, and widely informed. Although his arguments are his own, he was necessarily indebted to the ambience established earlier by Thomas Huxley. In his essay of the 1950s, for example, "Why I am not a Christian," Russell argued powerfully that Christianity had reversed the monastic ideal by linking religion and material prosperity in society: it paid to be a Christian. Russell found that the atheism of the past had been mean-minded and polemical, but that now it marked an intellectual elite for whom atheism was a form of boast. For him and many others, the debates of the past were irrelevant; if God was not dead, He was certainly moribund.

The effort to impose order on one's reading and lived reactions cannot reflect the erratic mouse-trails in the snows of experience that one so formlessly encounters in life. Among many influences, none had the clarity and power for me of George Santayana's writings on religion. I began reading him just before World War II and never stopped. He was born in Madrid in 1863 and baptized as a Catholic. Between ages nine and forty-nine, he lived in Boston as a boy, then in Cambridge, where at Harvard he was both student and finally professor of moral philosophy. Skeptical by nature and conviction, he attended Catholic services from his early days more as admirer than as believer. His earliest writings on religion were included and expanded in *Interpretations of Poetry and Religion* (1900). Here, and in his many later philosophical and autobiographical writings, Santayana revealed himself, to my reading, as a Catholic atheist, a position I found sympathetic and almost rational.

For Santayana, religious doctrines do not refer to matters of fact, since they are poetic, the work of the imagination, not a product of revelation. In his development of that idea, I found a bridge between the age-old logic chopping about God, and an imaginative grasp of the issues. Santayana wrote that the proper task of religion is to express an ideal, but when liberals seek to reinforce religion by forcing it into synchrony with popular, contemporary modes, its symbols are vulgar-

ized and impoverished. Hence, I thought, the contrast between medieval and renaissance painting and architecture, and the hideous painted
plaster saints of modern Catholicism, housed in churches outstanding
only for their inappropriateness. And the contrast between the Latin
mass and the current baby-talk translations of it played out before a
background of "I'm Hangin' Out With Jesus" on a guitar, was appalling. Santayana did not oppose religion, as do the ideologists of atheism, but he continued to insist on the moral function of the imagination and the poetic nature of religion. Without poetry and religion our
history would have been even darker than it is. Without imagination
the soul is chilled, and even clear perceptions of truth remain deprived
of joy and "the impetuosity of conviction." As he became fully grounded
in materialism and in his conviction of our animal nature, Santayana
would modify his humanism of 1900, but he never abandoned his
early position concerning the aesthetic origins of religious observance,
whether Catholic, Buddhist, or Hindu.

As for mysticism, Santayana described it as contrary to reason, and
the mystic's purpose was not to improve human nature but to eliminate it. At base, Santayana's position is that the human being is in
nature, natural, and set apart from the animal only by the chance of
evolution which endowed him with thumbs and a large brain. Nature
itself offers vast scope to imagination and understanding: no need to
look for wider vistas unless we are unwilling to endure "the sadness
and discipline of the truth."[4] That wider vista, that truth, is Santayana's
conclusion that God does not exist, and that the idea of God results
from men's efforts to blunt the hard edges, to counter the blows that
existence in uncaring nature leads us to.

In Santayana's psychology, the understanding is inadequate to the
task of interpreting and verifying data. Thus he remained skeptical
about the ambitions of scientists of his time to explain nature in its
entirety. The very weakness of the understanding forces the imagination to fill in gaps: "The intuitions which science could not use remain
the inspiration of poetry and religion." To the religious orders, such
intuitions were not called that, but prophecy or revelation, while some
philosophers call it "a higher reason." Adherence to the unreason of

---

4. George Santayana, *Interpretations of Poetry and Religion, The Works of George
    Santayana*, Triton Edition, 15 volumes (New York: Charles Scribner's Sons, 1936–
    1940), Vol. 2, p. 21.

prophecy or revelation in turn produced religious fanaticism in all its dire consequences, early and late in the historical record. Santayana wrote that fanaticism "consists in redoubling your effort when you have forgotten your aim."[5]

Although the Humanists tried to claim him, Santayana declined, saying that Humanism is a taste rather than a system, "and those who make a system of it are obliged to explain away what is not human in the universe as a normal fiction." He stood apart from humanistic agnosticism, seeing it, I believe, as intellectually indolent and falsely humble, a hedging of the Pascalian wager. He rejected Irving Babbitt's and Paul Elmer More's New Humanism of 1919 and later, finding it genteel, its alleged Platonism spurious because harnessed to Christianity.

I found Santayana's Catholic atheism further convincing because his naturalism, made luminous by his doctrines of essence, matter, truth, and spirit (in *Realms of Being*), reinforced my own experience by its liberating toughness, and because I see in it, as in his own final days, the essence of tragedy. He often commented on his delight in liberation from religion into indifferent nature, a liberation that offered the balance essential to the refinement and perfection of his philosophy. It is hard but not brutal, logically consistent, dignified without pomposity, and blessedly free of jargon. In the belief of death as final lies the possibility of enhanced pleasure in life itself, and further freedom from the illusion of life eternal. It has been said[6] that biblical faith "is never destroyed by tragedy but only tested by it, and in the test it both clarifies its own meaning and conquers tragedy." Here tragedy seems to mean simple mischance; the atheists' view of life as rich in possibility, necessarily filled with struggle and completed in the finality of death, is indeed, in the ancient Greek sense, tragic. Christian "tragedy," with its doctrine of resurrection, may be seen as a violation of the very meaning of tragedy. Santayana, dying of cancer at age eighty-nine, refused attempts of his nursing nuns to bring about a deathbed reconversion; he refused the sacrament of Extreme Unction; and his dying words were, "My only pain is physical."

In the United States, attitudes toward religion have changed since

5. George Santayana, *Reason in Common Sense* [1905] (New York: Charles Scribner's Sons, 1936), Triton Edition, Vol. 3, p. 22.
6. Emil J. Fackenheim, "On the Eclipse of God," *Commentary*, June, 1964.

World War II. Formerly it was widely assumed, apart from a few fundamentalists, that religious observance was "a collective make-believe." It was socially acceptable to indulge in a genteel hypocrisy, or to agree with Russell and others that atheism was automatic among the educated elite. With the shifting of sexual and other mores in the 1960s and 70s came the odd Californian move to quasi-religious movements, some exotic and some conventional. Established religions set about retranslating and vulgarizing the Bible, together with encouraging breaches in traditional dogma and procedure. The Catholic Church was found to be served by a widely publicized hypocritical clergy: accused of buggery and more straightforward seduction, the sinners were not excommunicated but sent for psychiatric counseling; the former counselors became the counseled. A Catholic observer would write, "When the sacred profession is perceived as perverted in America, louche in Ireland and both corrupt and stupid in Italy, it is a miracle that any conscientious young men join it at all."[7] Despite that, all denominations flourished as never before. The extreme right found religion again, noisily reborn in Christ, and antipathy to atheism took on a different aspect.

To the unreflective, atheism had always been suspect. The atheist was unreliable, his word in law merely an affirmation unconfirmed by oath on the Good Book. A whiff of Tourneur's atheist, d'Amville, of *The Atheist's Tragedy* (1611) remained in the late twentieth century still attached to atheism, in a subterranean Jungian manner. In the final act, the villainous d'Amville beheads himself (how?) in rage and bafflement at Charlemont's, the Christian hero's, meekness and long suffering in the face of treachery and his own imminent death. That same unreflective person would have approved of G.K. Chesterton when he wrote that Thomas Hardy "became a sort of village atheist, brooding and blaspheming over the village idiot." Chesterton's scorn was the rule, not the exception. The atheist was an outlaw, willingly set apart from the accepted blessings and responsibilities of decent people.

Now in the ultimate chapter of my education, I have learned that you may let it be known that you are a Gnostic, a Manichean, a Branch Davidian, a Mahayana Buddhist, a Nudist, or a believer in the sanctity of bumble bees, and people are likely to smile approvingly and ask how you got that way. But if by misfortune it should come out

---

7.   Charles Glass, *Spectator* , London [February 12, 1994], 14.

that you are not an agnostic but an atheist, you will meet either silence or a tolerant smile and an abrupt change of subject. I find that entirely as it should be, for ideological atheists, like ideological anybodies, are dangerous bores and death to sane discourse. Atheism has been preached zealously for more than 200 years in the West. While I consider atheism to be valid, I would prefer an atheistic-Trappist silence in place of noisy, hubristic defiance. Let us live and let live in Wallace Stevens's "old chaos of the sun," without transcendental illusion, knowing that we have no alternative. Religion, alas, teaches some of us neither how to live, nor how to die. As for Catholicism, I think often of a fellow Catholic atheist who, upon hearing of papal reforms remarked, "I want the Church I left to stay exactly as it was when I left it."

3

Sea-Going

I move back in time to another phase of my education: the Great Depression. I found it to be well-named, for it produced great depressions in man and boy alike. To my biased view, the Midwest, *l'Amérique profonde,* that expanse of flat land, flat speech, and flat-spirited people, prepared the mind for departure elsewhere, anywhere, that with luck might turn into permanent escape. For very young boys, escape took the form of constructing model airplanes and hiking out to the nearest airfield to watch proceedings. The exploits of World War I pilots, or of civilians such as Lindbergh, supplied arguments and even agreement among us boys in lazy summer hours on end. That background would lead many to flight training in the Army Air Corps or in the Navy. For some it would also lead to early death in what we came to call "our war."

Although I, too, cut out and glued balsa wood and rubber-band propelled bi-planes, and read my share of prose about aviation, flying seemed second-rate when compared with images of life at sea, and for a reason: when I was five years old, my uncle Ernest gave me the present of a ten-minute spin in a bi-plane over the town and surroundings of Wisconsin Rapids. The pilot was a friend of my uncle's, an itinerant who was trying to make a living from the two-dollar rides. His plane smelled of vomit, it was all hard metal edges, noisy and cold, and I could hardly see the earth over the cockpit. Flying was no fun; I preferred my memorable ride on the elephant, or the tame, predictable daily motion of the iceman's horse.

I cannot recall how the idea of the sea first came into my mind.

After the World War, my uncles had complained about the miseries of the transports they had ridden to France; otherwise no one I knew had gone to sea or had been a sailor. Early in my reading career, however, I came on Dana's *Two Years before the Mast,* and not long after a children's version of Melville's *Moby Dick* from which the interludes of natural history had been deleted (I was indignant when I discovered the original, satisfyingly long and detailed, full of wonderful lore). I turned up Marryat in the town library, where I prowled the shelves looking for books about the sea. One Saturday a suspicious lady librarian wanted to know what I was doing in the adult book section. She was accustomed to boys (and girls) seeking out medical books and any other anatomical treatises of potential prurient interest. But in the fullness of my years, the sea was now my pornography, my distant love.

The Depression inflamed my sense of the blankness, the flatness and the hopelessness of my native Midwest, and those years also intensified my longing to go to sea. At one point, I had aspired to Annapolis and a career in the Navy, but my father and others assured me that without a congressman's backing and influence I hadn't a chance. I might as well hope for a recommendation from the Holy Trinity. Necessity and my romantic ideal of the sea brought me to New Orleans in early June, 1936, where I went to work as a fry-cook in a place just off Canal Street.

The waitress told me that the man I replaced had got drunk and threatened to shoot the owner's wife. By the end of the first week, I could understand why. Emigrés from up-country Louisiana and in late middle age, neither the boss nor his wife had the vaguest idea of how to run the restaurant which they had bought with their lifetime savings, nor how to treat employees. New Orleans was not the place in which to serve up their country messes, or the fiercely awful coffee. They never went to the market for fresh produce, but bought cases of gallon-sized canned foods because they were cheap. A session over a gas-fired steel grill reduces the appetite to near-zero, yet the wife would stand over my shoulder as I served myself a meal at the end of a long stint, to make sure that I consumed no more than she thought correct. Grandly, they named the place "The Paradise," but I found it limbo or the inferno. It was soon obvious that "The Paradise" would go belly up; another dead-end job to add to my tally. Over-cooked stew and ten dollars a week were hardly enough to slide by on. Walking back to my room at night, I knew I reeked of grease, a nastiness that persisted no matter how thoroughly I scrubbed.

At least New Orleans was not Minnesota, and I was edging nearer to the sea. I reflected that I had been born in northern Minnesota, just south of the Canadian border where the Mississippi rises, and eighteen years later, here I was where it debouched into the Gulf of Mexico; perhaps I could take heart from that. The great wide river slid by, fast and noiseless, like red oil, laden with the erosion of Southern soils in its passage. At eighteen, I had not learned to observe: I looked but I did not see. New Orleans was only a partial revelation to me. Compared with any place I knew, it was exotic and attractive. It put to shame the frame bungalows and pretentious fakery of downtown Minneapolis, but it was no more than a series of semi-impressions. I looked at but did not see the wrought-iron *rejillas* (grills) and railed balconies in the French Quarter. I knew nothing of architecture and had never been to an exhibit of modern art. A few old masters I had seen only in reproduction. I had heard chance bits of baroque and romantic music on radio, but I knew nothing of its history and techniques. From years as an altar boy, I associated flowers with weddings or funerals. Any sensibility I possessed was severely literary, while my ambitions were fired only by negativity. A reluctant barbarian, I knew that I did not want to spend my life as a casual laborer, a cook, or a factory hand, but beyond wanting to go to sea, I did not know how to go about it. Dull labor dims both mind and eye. I had little free time, I worked ten to twelve hours a day, I made no friends.

After the brief suppertime rush, the waitress would leave, and I would work the grill and serve the results at the counter: cook, waiter, and cashier. Sometimes a merchant seaman would come in, giving me a chance to ask about prospects for a job aboard a ship. I knew that trouble was threatening on the docks. The National Maritime Union was trying to organize New Orleans; I had seen fist fights and heard rumors of knifings. A cop near the docks ordered me to "get the hell out of here." The U.S. merchant navy was in even worse shape than industry as a whole; it hardly continued to exist after its brief prosperity in the World War. "Only a damn fool would want to go to sea now, my boy," one old drunk told me, and I thought he was probably right. I had no papers and no experience, apart from cooking to qualify me, however meagerly, for a berth in a ship. I considered going back north to look for a construction job somewhere or other.

Foul weather, dripping humidity, and foul moods in the "Paradise": I had about decided that I was in the wrong place at the wrong time, and I gave notice to my enemy, the boss's wife, and to my landlord that I would be leaving in a week's time. A few days before my release from hamburgers and fried egg sandwiches, release in another form took shape.

Paul Bouvier had been a French naval cadet before 1914, and during the war had served as a junior deck officer in a cruiser. He had intended to make a full career in the Navy, but some kind of trouble— he implied involvement with an admiral's daughter, or possibly wife— forced him to resign and to transfer into the merchant navy. Shipping in France was in no better shape than it was in the U.S., and Bouvier had endured hungry intervals ashore. Rumors of berths in tankers, which the Mexicans were going to take over from the Americans, proved vaguely correct, and he ended up as first mate in a tanker I shall call *Guadalajara* .

Bouvier came into the restaurant late one night for a sandwich and a coffee. His English was worse than my stiff and limited French, but when I spoke to him in his language he was relieved and perhaps pleased. A tall, thin man with a small moustache and abundant black hair, he reminded me of my uncle Dan, except for the moustache. His ship was in port to pick up spare parts and to load deck cargo for Barcelona. What was I doing in New Orleans? I explained, and summoning courage, asked if he needed a man in the galley. When the boss turned up to count the till and lock up, Bouvier and I left together; he offered me a beer in a nearby bar. Scanty cash makes for abstinence. I had rarely drunk alcohol of any sort, but coupled with Bouvier's interest in my confused affairs, that beer tasted better than any drink since. He went to his ship, I to my room, and as we moved off in opposite directions, he called me back to say he would see what could be done about my coming aboard.

I felt a preliminary mixture of relief and jubilation, but riding the freights had taught me skepticism and the patience needed to wait for the event: an empty moving in the right direction before I could breathe easy. This time the train was going my way. In short order Bouvier took me to the purser to sign me on, arranged for apprentice seaman's papers, and sent me to the ship's cook, a slovenly Irishman who set me to peeling potatoes. Before sailing I had to buy shoes, dungarees, shirts, foul weather gear, and a sea-bag, so exhausting my savings. In

Guadalajara I would earn even less than at the "Paradise," but I would have shipped out for nothing if need be.

My first month aboard was a happy nightmare. I knew that I would have a lot to learn, but hadn't a realistic notion of how much or of how exacting the course would be. Although she flew the French flag, there was some connection to the Mexicans I never understood and did not think it wise to inquire. A year later I read that the Mexicans under Cárdenas had nationalized the oil industry, and I deduced that the ship must have been leased in some under-the-table manner from the French, with the understanding that a Mexican would technically be in command. Bouvier in fact ran the ship. The Mexicans were not noted as deep-water seamen; our "master," who had never commanded anything larger than a coastal fishing vessel, sat in his cabin playing solitaire, smoking cigars, and signing such papers as the purser put in front of him. The forty-man crew were assumed to speak Spanish, but we were so various in nationality and language that English or French predominated.

I began making lists in French and Spanish of seagoing terms I should know. Bouvier kept his necessary distance from the crew, but every now and then he would ask me to his cabin, where patiently he would answer my questions. In return I gave him English lessons and corrected his pronunciation. He also let me borrow his books, Balzac and Zola. He had said that he would transfer me out of the galley as soon as he could, but in the meantime I was to keep my eyes open and learn everything I could about the ship and seamanship. When I wasn't lugging provisions for Leary, the cook, I was swabbing the galley deck or making sandwiches for the night watch. I made friends with the boatswain (*contramaestre, maître d'équipage*), who began to teach me the most common knots and the difficult craft of splicing wire rope. Promptly I began to recognize how arrogant I had been to think that I could just pick up seamanship. More than a series of easily learned twists and turns, it was a way of life that would take a long lifetime to master.

Maps had always fascinated, but now my fascination turned to navigational charts. The quartermaster (*timonel, maître de manoevre*), an English-speaking Pole, had received a fresh set of Atlantic and Mediterranean charts, on which he spent hours with dividers and parallel rulers, plotting in corrections accumulated since their publication some years previously. Bouvier would permit me to come up to the bridge to see what went on in the mysteries of celestial navigation. That baffled me, for I had failed geometry in high school, while algebra and trigonometry were unfathomable. Bouvier's sextant, in its suede leather case, however, was a beautiful object, and I hoped one day to possess and to use my own counterpart.

Before going aboard, I was anxious about my reception by the crew; would they hate my guts, or what? To my relief, most of them ignored me, some like the boatswain were kind and patient, but more than a few showed contempt for an ignorant young gringo, as indeed I was. I felt that I was continually on trial and probably failing it (a feeling that stayed with me for many years). I was to find out that in all ships the divide between the engineers and the deck crew was unbridgeable. In *Guadalajara* the engineers lived in oil-reeking squalor and were proud of it, but Bouvier insisted on minimal sanitation and inspected our mephitic quarters every ten days or so. He also ran fire and abandon-ship drills. Some muttered at his discipline, but they respected him, as opposed to our captain, a nonpresence, not even a figurehead. Our ignorance of one another's language was a barrier, but one I could shelter behind while I tried to find my sea-legs, survive the trial. The longer I was aboard, the more impressed I was at the competence of most of the crew. There was no place for bluff or phoniness. A seaman had to know his job, whatever his other failings might be.

Memories of that distant time are unreliable, treacherous. My notebook of that time, irregularly kept, went up in flames during World War II, but vividly present in memory are the first days at sea, the sea itself that I had wanted so fiercely to feel beneath the deck of a ship. The sea I first set eyes on after a slow, foggy trip to the mouth of the Mississippi was of course the Gulf of Mexico. In the early, hot morning it was placid, lake-like if not swamp-like, and I felt cheated. It was not until we rounded Florida and moved into the Atlantic proper that I was reassured. The sodden atmosphere of New Orleans lay far behind, the memory and smell of it cleansed by a stiff breeze, the sun high, unobscured by the few cumulus clouds on the horizon. A moderate sea gave life, independent motion, to our rust-streaked decks. Released from the galley for an hour, I inhaled salt air and felt alive as never before. A loaded tanker carries little freeboard, therefore even a moderate sea will occasionally break over the deck, an effect that surprised and delighted me. I was at home, whatever that might mean, as never on land since early childhood. That first pleasure in deep green water, heightened in high seas and storms, never left me; I reacted to the sea as Saint-Exupéry reacted to flying. Only in the years of escorting convoys in the war was that joy in the sea clouded by the continuous necessity for alertness.

A few days into the voyage I was emptying garbage cans over the stern, desecrating the green sea, when Leary came up from the galley to say I was to report to the bridge. I cleaned myself up hastily, praying to God that Bouvier was fulfilling his promise to bring me up on deck. He was. From that day on, I was liberated from Leary's bitching, from wrestling boiling pots and from breathing the stifling galley air. Now it was chipping rust, swabbing oil spills that the engineers seemed to create deliberately, and eventually standing a wheel watch, which I found the best job of all. The science of holding the ship to a given compass bearing had to be learned from observing the old hands, and after frequent cursings-out by the mate: "Madre de puta, hombre, donde vas?" An instinct for how the ship would behave in a following sea or with the sea abeam had to be developed, and all too slowly I developed it. An old seaman always took the helm during drills, when we were in close waters, and while docking or undocking. Simply to be topside in the air and to be able to see how the ship was run from the bridge was exhilarating.

A ship's company forms an unusual society. Its definition is at once obvious and obscure, clear and opaque. I soon became conscious of two hierarchies: one obvious, rigid in terms of rank, experience, and responsibility. The other was unspoken, subtle, and subject to bulges and lurchings. These two orders of hierarchy were played out in the smaller grouping of engineers, who affected to despise the deck sailor, a view the deck heartily reciprocated. I became dimly aware of the stratification over time, but only dimly; I was a greenhorn with a lot to absorb. Certain facts forced themselves upon me when I came up on deck out of the galley. I had become unclassifiable owing to the first mate's favoring me, therefore suspect by many, uneasily held in minor awe by others, and someone to be avoided by almost all. In the galley I was nameable, easily put in a compartment, and eventually, if I did not disgrace myself, would have been given my full place in the order of things. The boatswain had enough rank and earned authority to ignore the general suspicion of me, but he could not appear over-friendly to an unformed youngster without the risk of rumblings about his motives and a resultant slippage in his authority.

One boiling July afternoon five of us were slowly paying out the anchor chain on deck and wire-brushing it. It was hot work, and the others were bare to the waist. I kept my shirt on because my fish-belly white skin burned easily, peeled, and burned again, never turning brown. A little German alongside me, his bronzed torso covered in hair, stared at my shirt and said, "Du bist schwul, nicht?"

"Comprends pas." I went on working. I knew no German, but it was obvious that he wasn't paying me a compliment.

"He wants to know," someone interpreted, "if you're a fruitcake."

"Fruitcake?"

"Yeah, a pansy, a bugger."

I was rattled and angry, so much so I couldn't answer the German, couldn't get out a straight thought or any of the blood-curdling answers I made later in my mind. "Don't let it eat you, kid," the interpreter said. "Your trouble is you don't look like a seaman. You look like someone in an office."

That annoyed me as much as the German's insult. I wanted to be a seaman and to look like one; the revolting idea of life in an office made me think of my father and all his pretensions. A fair skin and book-reading had damned me. I longed to look old and controlled, not young and confused.

I vaguely knew then, and later specifically knew of the reputation among landsmen of seamen as practicing homosexuals. At eighteen, homosexuality to me was a fact, but unreal in spite of the "wolf" in a boxcar when I first went out on the road. Sexuality as a whole was not a subject tolerated in conversation among decent people, and in my limited experience, even people deemed indecent, workingmen and seamen, were restrained on the whole. Dirty jokes would make the rounds, but for us in school they had no more reality than the perversions we pored over in Krafft-Ebing and Havelock Ellis. The men in *Guadalajara,* and with a sole exception, the sailors I knew very well at sea in the Navy, were ragingly heterosexual. If homosexual, and statistically some must have been, they were secretive about it. At eighteen I was no longer heterosexually innocent, but the remnants of a Catholic education were a partially effective coolant, and like many others, fear of disease and a priggish fastidiousness kept me out of brothels and casual encounters. "You're not a man until you've had a dose of clap," was the boast and cliché among men I worked alongside in those years.

The common attitude to women was confusing. The same man who bragged about his dose might have "Mother" tattooed on his chest. Women were revered, feared, chased for their favors by those who could shoot a line, as the slang among rakehells had it, and despised. I had always liked women and found them easier to talk to than men, and many I knew later in university became good friends rather than potential bed-partners. The unspoken code was that you did not sleep with a girl whom you would not willingly marry, and our poverty was such that marriage was for a remote, unimaginable future, if ever.

Mid-Atlantic, and one noon the messing compartment was full of rumor that we were not headed for Barcelona after all. New orders were for Algeciras, some said, others claimed it would be Alicante or Malaga. No, an old hand said, not Alicante: no facilities for discharging cargo there. Finally Bouvier announced to all hands that we would put into Marseilles for additional deck cargo, then unload at Malaga and take on ballast for return at best speed to Tampico. The Spanish Army in Morocco had revolted and it looked as though civil war was breaking out.

The news sent ripples of excitement among the crew. The French looked forward to shore time in their own country, but the Spanish became preoccupied. Off watch they would haunt the radio shack for news of any uprising and debated what civil war would mean to their relatives. Several hands were Andalusian, but the engineers were mostly from Bilbao or from small towns in the Basque country. The change in temperature in the crew impressed upon me the difference between how the war news affected the personally concerned Europeans and how it struck me, an ignorant and unconcerned American. Soon I felt increasing concern at my shipmates' reactions, as unsettlingly confusing news filtered through to us. I well realized that my ignorance, hardly relieved by high school courses in European history and geography, was extensive. I knew nothing of politics in the abstract, nor did most of the crew, come to that, but I lacked their practical and personal involvement in the political crisis taking shape. It was a source of further estrangement from them, creating for me a sensation of guilty isolation from what so totally mattered to them. Comprehension of the enlarging ball of concern in the bellies of the Spanish was not aided by linguistic confusions and the increasing tempo of foreign speech shooting past me.

Moving slowly into Marseilles harbor and anchoring after ten days at sea in itself was a pleasure; in the early morning light mist, the sight of the city in the distance almost made me weep. It would be my first taste of Europe, more than a place I had longed to see for as long as I could remember, as an ideal, a vision. We had no sooner dropped both anchors than Bouvier passed the word that we would load cargo from a lighter, and there would be no shore leave for anyone. The French sailors swore, and I wanted to. I felt like a child invited to a party but turned away at the door. We were no more than eight hours there, lying well off the shallow inner harbor, but teasingly near that fine waterfront, flanked by the hillside rising above the old city (which would be dynamited by the Germans), all of a piece in texture and color. We loaded ten wooden cases stenciled ROUAGES (gears), and heavy.

"Nah, guns. Bullets," Casimir, the Polish quartermaster said, and no one contradicted him.

We got under way in the twilight, and Jacobs, an American who bunked near me, grumbled, "We ain't being paid to go in no war zone." Usually he ignored me, which was all right with me. At age thirty he looked fifty, from drink and who knows what else, but he was a good signalman and could spell the radioman when called on. He had pretty good street Spanish.

"You think we're really going into a war?"

"Maybe not a war, but not a tea party, neither. Last night we got reports about air raids."

"Air raids on what?"

"They said 'centros communistas.' Whatever that means."

I reconstruct our exchange from the traitor, memory, but I am sure it is 90 percent accurate. The idea of a war zone was exciting. This is what the sea had brought me, real life among real events, relief from the monotony of life ashore. It is hard to explain how long it took us, in those years, to realize what the issues were in the Spanish Civil War. I saw only moments in a badly shot newsreel and heard only prejudiced, personal comment from the few Spaniards aboard, inarticulate men and little better equipped than I was to interpret the fragments of fragments we witnessed. (So it would be in November, 1943, off Tarawa. We heard vaguely of German misadventures in the Soviet Union, but that news meant exactly nothing to us; we were concentrated on what was one Christ-awful mess for the Marines ashore.)

I had seen nothing of Bouvier after our change of destination, and when finally I had a chance to speak to him, he said he couldn't discuss the ship's movements. When he could, he would do so. Under way for Malaga, slightly but significantly the crew changed habits and attitudes. What had been simply work took on purpose, although what purpose no one put into words. On lookout we began really to look out, to examine the skies as well as the stretch of waters to the horizon in our sectors.

Malaga was a surprise. I thought it might be little more than a fishing port; one of our Andalusians had a brother who fished out of there. The sheer beauty of the bay of Malaga could not be ignored, nor the lion-colored mountain range in the near distance, shimmering in the heat. Far from being from a mere fishing port, it was the second port in Spain after Barcelona, someone told me, and equipped to discharge our cargo all too rapidly. Bouvier wanted to get away fast. Black smoke arose about a mile or more beyond the port area, to which we seamen were confined by half a dozen ragged militia, some barefoot, armed with shotguns or hunting rifles. They said they were loyal to the government, that a fascist plane had dropped a bomb, perhaps more than one, the day before, killing an old grandmother and a baby. They wanted to give us black tobacco cigarettes; I gave them a tin of pipe tobacco, and Bouvier told Leary to send them a ham. The stevedores were delighted at our deck cargo from Marseilles. They patted the wooden cases as though they were obedient horses, and one of them kissed the case as he maneuvered it into position on a truck. I liked these people; I wanted to see more of them, but it would be years before I would see anything of Spain but that port from a ship, and that, to me, extraordinary dockside.

On our second trip to Malaga several weeks later, the atmosphere had changed. Beyond doubt the city was on a war-footing. Men who had formed a rag-tag militia not long ago were now in more or less similar uniforms. Some had been under fire north of Madrid; they described efforts to fight with small arms against heavy artillery and planes. By then I had read everything I could get my hands on about Spain. I learned the issues at stake, and I wanted to be there and to join the Loyalists. Bouvier said I was an idiot and to forget it.

Back in dusty Tampico, Bouvier was about to leave the ship and return to France. I realized that it was time for me to leave, too. It was time for university, but I still wanted to find out whether I could arrange a trip back to Spain. I had read about the formation of the Lincoln Brigade, then in January, 1937, of the fall of Malaga to the Italian artillery and tanks. I told myself that I "loved" Spain, a phrase from books, and from the impressions of a naïf. By the time I discovered that to get to Spain I would have to sign up not only with the Communist Party but with the Stalinist stripe of communism in New York City, my latent skepticism took over. Worse still, it had become obvious that Franco and his German and Italian fascist allies were winning the struggle. I was too young, I had been too ignorant, and it was too late.

4

The Romans in Athens: Salzburg and Berlin

Two attics enriched my childhood in central Wisconsin. My grandfather's was littered by a pair of football cleats, flowered hats, two round-top wooden and metal trunks, a torn Douay Bible, and the battlefield trophies that my uncles had brought back from France. The second attic was in my aunt Elizabeth's house, a few blocks up the hill from my grandfather's. Similar objects lay about that attic, but the prize was a Springfield bolt-action 30/30, complete with bayonet, with which my aunt's husband had soldiered in Cuba in 1898. My cousin Bob, a year younger than I, would be shepherded down the hill to play with me, and we would make for the attic, which was either baking hot or arctic cold, to put on the gas masks, which smelled of rotting rubber, and one of us would wear the German helmet, a spike on top and a murderous dent on one side. Aided by the illustrated war history in the living room, we formed romantic and approximate notions of trench warfare, which sometimes in good weather we would enact outdoors. Later in Illinois at about age ten, I would organize my neighborhood friends into Americans and Germans, omitting in our patriotic ignorance the French and the British. We dug trenches in an empty building-lot and heaved at one another hand grenades made of sods. Entire Saturdays passed in such warfare, interrupted only by a truce for lunch.

I would harry my uncles with questions about the war; normally they were articulate about banal hometown topics, but they were unwilling to open up about the war. Mainly I learned that *boches* was a bad word, and Germany a distant and ugly place of barely human inhabitants. Ernest would only drop hints about the war, as did Henry.

49

Nestor was silent, but his silence was expressive, almost explosive, about Germany, where he had been stationed for several months in the army of occupation. By the time I was in university and went to Wisconsin in summers looking for work, Nestor had mellowed and would hesitatingly recall pleasant memories of this post-combat duties as occupier in 1918–1919. None of my uncles thought in abstractions or questioned our having entered the war; they showed none of the bitterness of the French or the British about its waste and futility. Ernest, the most intelligent of the brothers, did assume a skeptical attitude toward the end of his life, I think, but he died before I was old enough to discuss the war with him.

One result of all that was a growing fascination with matters German, just as after World War II, some of the young sported swastikas and other Nazi regalia. The implicit dilemma led to study of German as a minor subject in university, an unpopular choice among my friends after the bombing of Guernica and the triumph of Franco in the Spanish Civil War. In 1940 we followed the bombing of England and the desperation of the RAF hourly and daily on radio and in the press, believing that our country would and should enter the war promptly. No political or ethical conviction, however, reduced my pleasure in German lyric poetry and German music: a fine world of art was there, having nothing to do with the prevailing ambience of arrogance and barbarism, nationalism gone berserk.

Naval service in the Atlantic and Caribbean did nothing to endear Germany to me. Sailors and officers alike showed distaste for the Germans, but nothing stronger than distaste; most of us had learned to doubt tales of atrocities in the first war. It was not until 1945 that we knew of the concentration camps and horrors transcending atrocity. If anything the newsreels, films, and authenticated accounts of survivors of the camps increased my curiosity about Germans and emphasized the strangeness of their civilized accomplishments existing cheek-by-jowl with savagery.

In 1951, Ph.D. finally in hand, I found bearable teaching jobs in the U.S. scarce to nonexistent, but I was lucky enough to get a place in Austria on the staff of the recently founded Salzburg Seminar in American Studies. It had been organized through the efforts of F.O. Matthiessen, professor of English at Harvard, and an Austrian refugee student. Their rationale was that Europeans had been cut off from American intellectual life by the war, and in many countries by censorship and governmental intransigence for years before the war. At Schloss Leopoldskron, Salzburg, several lengthy sessions a year took place, principally in literature, history, and politics, attended by continental and British writers, academic people, and an occasional civil servant. As one of the small resident staff, I was to lecture in my areas of competence, to suggest American faculty for invitation, and to travel about Europe to interview candidates for future seminars, a pleasant duty shared with the resident director. Like generals, we divided the map of Western Europe between us.

Leopoldskron, the eighteenth-century rococo palace of the Bishop of Salzburg, had come into the impresario, Max Reinhardt's hands, then by rental into ours. It was a shock to many of the participants to find that the threadbare splendor of the library and dining room contrasted with bare-board dormitory accommodations and too few toilets. The place had suffered from neglect during the war years; it operated on scanty funds throughout its early history. The Austrian staff of chef, under cooks, housekeeper, and numerous maids worked hard and were paid reasonably by the prevailing Austrian standards; the dollar bought many schillings, but not so many as the American donors believed. In contrast with the participants' accommodations, the apartments of the resident staff were palatial. My cash salary was laughable, but my quarters were more than adequate for my family, and on cold winter mornings, it was luxury to know that by six o'clock a maid would have built a fire in the towering tiled stove. American academic people of some eminence and an occasional poet or novelist lent credibility to our brochures, and we attracted, for a time, some of what might be called the rising cream of European intellectual life, most of whom were in their twenties or early thirties.

The lugubriously named "participants" were various. Some came simply for an Austrian holiday; some to get acquainted with recent American books, of which we had 15,000; some came to chase women; many came to study; several combined all such motives in differing measures. Almost all displayed distinction of one kind or another. One Swiss girl's distinction was of an individual variety: she spent her days lying in the sun, wearing a bikini, the first I had seen. She spoke to no one and regarded all of us with distaste, before succumbing to the blandishments of a small, dried-up professor of psychology, who was prepared to leave wife and child for her. The Schloss was a lively place and a welcome break from wartime austerity, especially for the

British, far into the peace. Beer was cheap as was the highly alcoholic, hangover-producing *Neuwein*, which was consumed copiously. Of an evening, people danced, causing my dachshund bitch, Anna, to nip their ankles. Through the days and nights, liberated from ordinary pursuits, people conversed and converged as never before. Enduring friendships were made; love affairs, mainly heterosexual, flourished; jealousy and anger flared, and more than one marriage dissolved in that charged atmosphere.

High drama and low comedy were played out summer and winter. At times I felt as thought I was in the chorus of an opera combining *The Barber of Seville* and *Tristan und Isolde*. In my second summer, an American poet arrived and proceeded to cut broad swathes through all green fields. Unknown to us, he was suffering from a bout of recurrent mania, a condition that kept him sweatily awake night and day, conducting frantic sessions on poetry, declaring his love and intention to marry a handsome *Milanesa* who was already engaged to an Italian poet; setting out to climb to nearby Berchtesgaden, Hitler's former hangout, but getting no farther than the Bierstube, where he held another informal seminar for all and sundry. The uproar lasted for a month. Just before the men in white coats arrived, he accused me of playing up to his wife, a lovely and talented woman whom I admired but assuredly had no designs upon. Greatly gifted and greatly afflicted, his antics caused untold troubles on all sides.

Distress of another kind touched the poet and editor, Karl Shapiro. Until he accepted our invitation to the seminar, he had never been in Europe, and as a Jew had never wanted to have anything to do with the Germans. Arriving by ship at Cherbourg, he had travelled by train to the German border, where the severe customs and immigration agents, concerned to prevent currency smuggling, thoroughly investigated each traveller. Shapiro said that when the train approached the German border, his heart was racing as uninvited gas-chamber scenes appeared before him; all he could think was that he must leave the train and return to the United States. Gradually mind dominated emotion and he made himself endure the routine questioning of the officials and forced himself to remain in the train. When I met him at the Salzburg station, he looked dreadful, gray in the face and distracted. Over the next few days he resumed the charming, skeptical manner that was authentically his.

Summer passed, and with cool weather came Saul Bellow, lugging what he called an "almost portable" typewriter on which he was writing *The Adventures of Augie March.* He at once bribed one of the maids to place a breakfast tray outside his door first thing in the morning, thus sparing himself the communal breakfast table. He would then type his daily stint and appear among us at mid-morning. One evening he read to the assembly the chapter in which Augie acquires a hunting hawk on his drive to Mexico; Bellow laughed without restraint at his own prose, causing the rest of us to laugh either with or at him. He played Mozart on the recorder expertly; he was one of the few people I knew who genuinely conversed, his talk glinting with intelligence, wit, and curiosity. He was pleased when I told him that in the course of a visit to I Tatti, I had praised his fiction to Bernard Berenson and had later sent him my copy of *Dangling Man* (Bellow's first novel).

Early in the sessions of the Seminar, national groups would troop together, but within a day or two, the groups would break up, owing to the director and his wife, who saw it as their duty to introduce people and to create a first-name, American atmosphere in the face of European well-mannered stiffness. The Germans above all arrived in stiffness but soon melted into a familiarity that could be alarming. Meals were taken at long pine tables. On one occasion early in a session, two Germans seated themselves among several Dutch. On learning their nationality, one German said "Ah. I well know your country. I was there with our army in the war." The Dutch arose silently, and as one moved off to find another table.

I had done no interviewing in Germany; thus I was keen to meet the Germans and to try to sift through the various and conflicting attitudes about their national character that I had met so often. I was uneasy with generalizations about national character, but life In Leopoldskron encouraged such thinking and often lent it a convincing validity. I liked the Germans' seriousness and sense of purpose, although both qualities could be overdone, as I would come to understand. It was clear that these intelligent people consciously bore the weight of their recent history. They resented that history, and in a subterranean manner, resented us, the victors. We presented them a map of the postwar world, one which they were forced to study and to follow. With less intensity, many of the French and British reacted similarly to American certainty about our country's economic and moral place in the postwar world. Time, to be sure, would put matters straight as to who had been the "winners" of that war.

Our housekeeper was a vigorous, gray-haired, managing sort of woman with a youthful complexion. Her husband was the former game-keeper of the area, "former" because he had been what his wife called a "*kleine Nazi*," one not prominent enough for trial in one of the allied courts, but sufficiently notorious to be forbidden to hold a civil service job. As in better days, he continued to wander about in Austrian native dress: knee breeches, a short green jacket and a black hat decorated with feathers. He was much taken by my Remington .12 gauge shot-gun, which I hoped to use the our small lake, little more than a pond but full of ducks. He, who had policed *Land* Salzburg with a weapon all his days, was forbidden to bear arms under the Allied de-nazification policy. He was deferential to me, but his deference had a contemptu-ous edge; I think he was puzzled by an American Herr Doktor who had arrived with a shotgun. Invited to the annual shoot through his influence with the local club, I embarrassed him when I knocked down only two ducks, in contrast to the many trophies each of the Salzburg burgers managed to bag. As for me, I found it ludicrous that we gentry sat on shooting sticks or stood idly at ease as the local farmers, in water to their navels, beat the reeds with sticks to force the ducks to fly past our assigned positions, there to be murdered: very different from rabbit and bird hunting in the Midwest or in New En-gland.

What with travel to countries that I had always longed to see, with trying to keep up with recent literature, on which I lectured; with meeting numbers of genuinely interesting and stimulating people; the Salzburg Seminar had been an unforgettable place. After a year and a half, nevertheless, I was ready for a change; I could not write there, for both occupation and stimulation forbade the time essential to time and reflection. It was all a great deal of fun, but fun could not pay for my father's upkeep back in Minnesota, nor did I take to the adminis-trative tasks that went with the job. We were told that no more money for books was forthcoming because the dining hall needed re-furbish-ing. The tenor of the experiment was changing; it was becoming insti-tutional, while emphasis on literature was giving way to social science and law. Literary people needed subsidy and were high-spirited, even disruptive. Not solid.

In another direction, I had gradually discovered from anti-American

remarks overheard at an outdoor café in Salzburg that the place was
less than endearing, for all its vaunted *Gemütlichkeit*. The source of
my disquiet, a 250-pound sweating fellow in greasy Lederhosen shouted
about the American Army of Occupation, "When the Russians come,
those fat-asses won't be able to escape, much less fight." To be sure, I
had had similar thoughts as I saw infantrymen driven to a field exercise by their wives or women in imported Chevrolets and Fords, but it
was not up to that Austrian to score the point. Similar remarks gained
their dubious authority in the *Salzburger Nachtrichten*, in which letters to the editor regularly registered outrage that their beautiful, Ger-
man-speaking Eden should be occupied by an American army, to say
nothing of their beautiful Leopoldskron, inhabited by Americans too,
those Romans in Athens. These were the judgments of little or not-so
little Nazis who had bought refuge in *Land* Salzburg when it had
become obvious that the war was not going so well; the hills were
alive not with the sound of music but with them.

Altogether such matters led me to accept an offer to go to both the
Free University and the Technical University in Berlin, where part-
time lectureships would add up to a full, if meager, salary. Those jobs
had been arranged by Douglas Blackett, the British Council representative in Berlin, who had attended a six-week session at Leopoldskron
in summer, 1952. As a captain in the Territorials, Blackett had been
taken prisoner in 1940, before the evacuation at Dunkirk, when his
unit had been cut off by the advancing Germans. He was a neatly put
together man, who affected a military moustache which made him
look older than he was, one year older than I. He came to my lectures
and we got on well. I asked him about his p.o.w. years, and he described life in eighteen different camps, from Austria and Bavaria and
up to Poland. He knew German well, respected the Germans, but not
the Austrians.

"Why is that?" We were walking along the lake for a beer at the
nearby Stube.

"The Austrians didn't give a curse about the Geneva Convention.
They intercepted our post, stole our packages, and bullied officers and
other ranks alike."

"Not so *gemütlich* ?"

"No, indeed. But the farther north we went, the better our treatment.
The Prussians followed the Geneva Convention to the letter. We shared

our packages with the guards, and they shared their rations with us, even when rations were pretty pitiful."

Blackett's was the first favorable report about the Germans I had heard, and from a man who had good reason to know what he was talking about. He said that when he learned of his posting to Berlin, he went to British Council headquarters in London and asked to see the Berlin file. It contained only one sheet, a memorandum from Rex Warner, the poet and novelist, which said, "Get me out of this place." Those words had given Blackett pause, but he had found Berlin far more compelling than had Warner. One chapter of my own life was falling apart in ways I need not recount, hence there was little to keep me in Salzburg. After a brief trip to Genoa and Milan to visit friends, I went to Berlin in early fall, 1952.

The contrast with *Land* Salzburg was total. In place of the neat foothills of the Bavarian alps and the dramatic mountains in the near distance, I found the sandy Prussian plains, then the bombed city, damaged on a scale and with a thoroughness no form of photography could convey. Salzburg had been untouched by bombing; Berlin was 90 percent destroyed. In the few years since the war, little had been done to reconstruct the city; the *Wirtschaftswunder* had yet to begin. In West Berlin, consisting of the American, British, and French sectors, at least much of the rubble had been cleared away, to form the "Berlin alp," as the locals called it. In the East, or Russian, sector, the rubble remained, hardly touched, it seemed, since the hour when the dust had settled after the carpet bombs, one by one, had exploded. Such acres upon acres of devastation were hard to grasp in any human manner. Would my commitment to Berlin be somehow inhuman also? I hated to think that it might be.

Feeling utterly defeated by the failure of my wartime marriage and the loss of my small son, whom in a sense I was abandoning, I was much cheered by the Blacketts' hospitality. Given a large house in the Grunewald by the largesse of the Occupation, they insisted that Anna and I should take over an unused apartment in their residence. I was embarrassed but relieved that they refused payment, for my salary from the part-time lectureships was far from ample. I was permitted to pay for the attentions of Frau Danziger, who made the long trip from East Berlin daily to work for the Blacketts. About fifty in age, she was cheerful and efficient, so much so that she emptied my desk drawers to dust them, then polished my shoes, the soles included. A crisis erupted when I forbade her to clean my desk or to polish the soles of my shoes. Frau Danziger wept, Anna barked, and I felt ashamed of my intolerance of her zeal. In time the German reputation for cleanliness became a mystery to me. Surfaces indeed shone, brasses were polished daily, but public rooms were pungent. In winter public buildings reeked of cheap tobacco, of a nasty wartime soap, of food, and of human sweat. No window was ever opened, since drafts were believed to bring disease as well as loss of precious heat. Even the buses were equipped with heavy felt curtains to keep out the cold air.

Another souvenir of the war was hunger, or its memory. In the United States then, no one ate food in public, apart from children licking ice cream cones, or munching hot dogs at ball games. In Berlin, people appeared to eat all the time. Herring stalls on the Kurfürstendam sold Rollmops on sticks to be eaten on the street at all hours. During the intervals of performances at the Komische Oper in East Berlin, the audience slowly paced the foyers, chewing rye bread sandwiches.

Such annoyances, as I judged them to be in my superior American way, dwindled to nothing in comparison with my admiration for how the Germans went about reconstituting their cultural life after the aesthetic absurdities of the Nazis. In East Berlin, the Komische Oper, resplendent and whole among the ruins, testified to the eagerness of the communist state, the Deutsche Demokratische Republik, to show its fidelity to a high cultural tradition. In West Berlin, the Deutsche Operoffered a full menu of traditional opera, not of the highest caliber, but a wonderful boon to the operatic novice I was. When I asked a friend why we heard so many over-aged singers, he explained that they were *Beamten* (civil servants) and by law were entitled to sing on until their retirement age. Anyway, for five marks I could see a performance almost every week of the season, and between times hear the superb Berlin Philharmonic, which had re-formed after the Hitlerian purge of Jews and was very much in business, first under Celibidache, then Furtwängler. Ironically, the allied commission had banned Furtwängler, but tolerated the Nazi Party member and true believer, Karajan, who took over in 1955.

Soon after the universities opened in the late fall, my lectures in American literature and history introduced me to some of the byways of the German system, and to acquaintance with the nature of the students. Having feared that the Technical University would be all technical, I found excellent faculties in music, art history, and languages, and students in those subjects as zealous as those in engineering or architecture. Specialization had not ruled out a good grounding in the arts, hence a numerous group in German society, not only in Berlin, were prepared to support the arts with subsidies as well as with attendance and participation. Eventually I decided that for many Germans, embarrassed by Nazism, a turn to their cultural tradition was a way of coping with recent history and rejoining Western society on even terms. Subsidies for the arts were good politics, but they were so because a large population approved of that politics and made it possible.

The Technical University benefited from having been long established; it also happened to be situated in the western sector, with the added advantage of support from the Occupation, later from the central government, in Bonn. The former University of Berlin, the Humboldt, was in the Russian sector and subject to Communist Party control, which proved stifling for all but the ideological enthusiasts. Partly as a skirmish in the cold war, the Ford Foundation among other agencies built from the ground up a new university named, challengingly, the Free, to offer noncommunist fare to the young of the city, and to the country at large.

Established in the suburb of Dahlem, in the American sector, the Free University had been hastily erected and staffed. Even though the American authorities in western Germany were busy imprinting our ways on German primary and secondary schools, through wisdom, good fortune, or intervention of the gods, they left the university system pretty much alone. American Institutes (departments) were set up, but they functioned within the traditional German structure: the faculties elected a rector from their body each year, who administered the institution with the aid of a dean or two and a small secretarial staff. Students were assumed to be adult; no counseling was provided, and mighty little advice. Bundles of red tape were eliminated by the fact that each entering student was issued a *Studienbuch*. As he attended lectures and seminars of his choice, he would present his book to the lecturer at the end of the course, which book the lecturer could sign or not, subject to the student's participation. When after x years the student thought himself ready for examination, he presented his book, paid a small fee, and was examined in his chosen area. Students were free to study in any German university; their wanderings would appear in the *Studienbuch*.

I found the system admirable. It meant that universities placed first emphasis on academic matters; that faculties remained responsible for academic decisions, and that students were regarded not as semi-delinquent children (although some were), but as responsible people capable of rational decisions (although some were not). Given that Berlin was an island in a political sea, surrounded by the Russian zone, the great majority of students were Berliners, Berlin born. They ranged in age from eighteen to the mid-twenties, which meant that they had known little previously but Nazism. Many of their parents had been either passive or active Nazis; many of their fathers were still prisoners of war in the Soviet Union. As long as I remained in Berlin, emaciated figures would turn up, one by one, having worked for years in Soviet mines or factories as virtual slaves. Every student had been marked by the war, by the bombing and occupation of his city. Several came to study with me not for my brilliant reputation, but in the hope of a scholarship to the United States.

Men outnumbered women by ten to one, but the women tended to be steadier and more responsible than the men. Perhaps the majority wanted to teach in the secondary school system. My subjects were not rooted in the standard English language and literature curriculum; thus I often had students with a genuine interest in what I was trying to teach, rather than a large body of people leaping hurdles en route to examinations. The attitudes of students were determined by the attitudes (and the attitudinizing) of the professoriat.

It is a truism that German order and consciousness of rank are highly developed, but one must live and work in that regimen fully to realize how letter-perfect that truism is. Some of the old boys whose experience extended back to the World War comported themselves like generals and expected to be regarded as such by colleagues inferior in rank and age. Younger faculty, many of whom had gone through the recent war, were more human in outlook and less buttoned up than the old guard, but not very much so. Relations between faculty and students hardly existed; like children, students were to be seen but not heard, unless in oral examinations. Office hours for students hardly existed. If a student had questions, he was expected to go to the professor's assistant, who might or might not satisfy the student's quest. Each institute had its own small library, kept under lock and key and as remote from students as possible. Lack of books was a serious difficulty, one responsible for the weakness, as I read it, of the lecture system: lecturers saw their task as providing facts for students to write down, word for boring word.

As a mere *Lehrbeauftrager* I had little occasion to mingle with the established faculty. When I did, I was greeted with chilly cordiality and freezing reserve. Naïvely, I failed to recognize for some time that Berlin was a gathering place for spies, and that newcomers were regarded as actual or potential spies unless or until it became clear that, innocently, they were what they were. I was neither spy nor black market profiteer nor currency dealer nor American triumphalist, unlike numerous others in that sad city, but I had to make my status plain by my work and way of life over many months before suspicions were relaxed, if not allayed. Because of my association with Blackett, a British official, many acquaintances believed that I was either on the American or British payroll rather than on a mean German salary. It was a fact that I played squash or tennis on facilities reserved for the allies; I could dine at the French club and drink in the British club, formerly the German tennis club, thus lending credence to suspicions that I was not on the up and up.

Those amenities made existence in Berlin more than bearable, but they set me apart from the Germans effectively. It was not that I wanted to be loved, as Saul Bellow had remarked, that all Americans abroad wanted to be: having saved the world single-handedly from Hitler, Mussolini, and Tojo, what else but love was their due? I simply wanted to learn what I could about how the Berliners lived and thought, how they saw their past and what they expected from the future. It was easier to talk to Herr Bieber, the local butcher who slipped Anna bits of choice trimmings, than to academic colleagues. The students who came to my lectures were another matter. I produced consternation one day when, fed up with their scribbling furiously as I spoke, I forbade them to take notes.

"I want you to think and ask questions, not sit there sponging up my words. If I said the sun had not risen his morning, you would write it down as correct. Let's have no more of that." I reserved time for questions and clarifications, but for weeks no one opened his mouth unless I forced a response from one victim or another.

"If I say something you do not fully understand, please stop me and say so. You'll be doing me a favor, and maybe others, too."

"How can we question what you tell us?" on student asked. "We are only students."

"Listen. I am not declaring holy writ here, I'm only setting up hypotheses about the past and suggesting to you some considerations about literature. Be skeptical. George Santayana said 'Knowledge begins in skepticism.' I think he was right."

Some were relieved, some were appalled, but after three months they began to unbend and lectures became less deadly for all of us.

Nine-tenths of the students had no money. Some lived with parents, if any; many worked at part-time or full-time jobs. State grants did not begin to cover their needs. One of my students, the best of the lot, worked as a bar-girl. I asked, "What is a bar-girl? Do you mix drinks behind the bar?"

"No, I sit in front of the bar. The men who come in, they talk to me, and my job is to get them to buy champagne."

She was not required to go off with the men, she assured me, and I wanted to believe her, but it seemed unlikely. It contradicted anything concerning the habits of what I had known as house girls. Fraülein Z. worked hard on assigned readings and was a pleasure in the lecture hall. She wrote excellent essays, turned them in on time and in English, unlike many who either wrote in German or in a kind of pidgin that was hell to read and correct.

As the cold, sodden winter came on, it was obvious that many students lacked adequate clothing. At one point I gave an old tweed suit to a first-year man, a refugee from the east who lived in one of the vast, unbearably crowded factory buildings provided for refugees while they were interrogated and "processed." He wore the suit every day, giving me a sense of unease approaching guilt. He spoke a great deal in class, too much, and made little sense. I had to wonder why he was studying, since he lacked both preparation and aptitude. Months later he left the university, but no one knew for what or where he had gone. He would be a refugee for life, I thought, the war never genuinely over for him.

June 17th, 1953, some weeks before the end of the summer term: a friend whose office was near the east sector telephoned me in mid-morning. He could see columns of smoke from his window and was hearing small arms fire. Something unusual was certainly happening; had I seen the morning papers? I had not, but it soon turned out that Berlin was seething with apocalyptic rumors: of a Soviet invasion, of the beginning of World War III. Many preposterous sounding reports would soon prove correct. East Berlin was afire; *Volkspolizei (Vopos)* and striking steel-workers from the mills at Henningsdorf, just over the border in the eastern zone, were skirmishing in Marx-Engels Platz, in Alexanderplatz, and even at the sector border in Potsdamer Platz.

Having cancelled my afternoon lecture, I stopped at Herr Bieber's to buy food for Anna. Herr Bieber said the late edition of *Abend* reported Russian troops from the zone in east Berlin in force. The radio confirmed that rioting was widespread. At midday I set out on foot for Brandenburger Tor, the traditional center for uprisings. The transport workers were on strike. The weather was hot, oppressive, and humid. The Brandenburg Gate lay beyond the bomb-rubble of the Tiergarten, which formed the boundary between the Russian and British sectors. In the Tiergarten, men bare to the belt and greasy with sweat were scything isolated patches of hay; the rest of the expanse was a growth of weeds and stunted trees, riddled by the bombs and shells of eight years before. Only the bombed-out bell tower, the Prussian Victory Memorial commemorating 1870, and the oversized statues of Moltke and Bismarck, badly chipped, remained to evoke Imperial Germany and the Prussia of pre-1848 (which had forbidden the citizenry to smoke in the Tiergarten).

In the Charlottenburger Chausee I joined a considerable crowd of West Berliners trudging to the border to see what was going on. Cars and bicycles moved even more slowly than pedestrians. Our column resembled refugees en route to a vague somewhere. It was an unusual mixture: shady-looking fellows, businessmen with their brief cases, young lovers, middle-aged married couples arm in arm; and the unmistakable refugees from the east, in clothes intended for others and expressions of patient dismay. It was an unusually quiet crowd, but not threatening. Some gestured toward the columns of smoke visible in the near distance; closer to the boundary, machine gun bursts further silenced the column. Several turned back, but most walked faster.

Since morning platoons of West Berlin police had tried to set up an orderly barrier, but randomly parked cars, the milling crowd, motorcycles and bicycles lying at uneasy angles among the police cars made for a barely contained chaos. One could hear gunfire from the direction of Potsdamer Platz, a mile or so away, but our area was quiet. Above the Gate, the familiar red flag was missing, replaced by the black-red-gold banner of pre-war, united Germany. American soldiers off duty took pictures with costly cameras; smartly dressed German women climbed on the roofs of cars to survey raw history through binoculars: shades of the onlookers at Waterloo in *Vanity Fair.*

As I pushed my way to within a few yards of the Brandenburger Tor, gunfire broke out just beyond it in the east sector. Now there were no cameras and no fashionable women. Here the crowd was made up of people from the east who had surged through the gate during the morning demonstrations. The men wore filthy pinstriped suits, black caps, and heavy shoes. They had the deeply browned faces not to be achieved on the tennis court but by hard manual labor. Small groups would knot together, armed with granite paving stones. I asked an old man smoking a cigar butt in a pipe who was doing all the shooting.

"Sehen Sie " (See for yourself), he gestured toward the gate.

I crossed over to the wide central arch, where the demonstrators shouted into the seemingly empty air. Elbowing to the front, I found what I half expected but was still astonishing: a Russian tank some thirty feet away, and six truckloads of Russian troops disposed tactically about the square separating the gate from Unter den Linden. Each truck mounted a light machine gun. Young boys were heaving stones at a Vopo hut until the nearest gunner opened fire on the gate itself, aiming just above our heads. I found myself on my belly, pressing one cheek into hot cobblestones, as did several men near me. Others had retreated behind the arch, while masonry dust settled. We joined them as the last man through the arch, a fat east German worker, jeered at us for running. He said the Russians didn't have the guts to shoot us down.

Machine-gun fire had changed the mood of the men near me. They had been scornful but good-natured, like a crowd at a football game. Now they were angry and roared to the Russians, *"Schluss"* (enough, knock it off). At the same time, boys would dart out from the barrier of the arches to stone the Russian trucks; they missed the trucks, but a volley hit the tank. The tank opened fire and the trucks joined in, aiming lower than before.

Only the young were rash; the men were of an age to have seen combat in the war. Age made them (and me) prudent. One boy, travelling fast, skidded head-first behind a column, like a rugby player scoring a goal. Blood was pumping from his thigh. His friends cut away his trouser leg with a jack knife as an ambulance pushed through, an attendant applied a tourniquet and loaded the victim aboard.

An unreal quiet followed, and one lost all sense of time. Before long, other adolescents approached the Russians, tormenting the crews by dangling cheap wrist watches and shouting *"Uhri, Uhri,"* pidgin Russian for "watches" and an insulting memory of the troops who had taken Berlin in 1945. Frozen-faced, the Russians squatted in their trucks. Boys harangued: how could you fire on working men? Finally a small captain hurried around the tail-board of one truck, produced his pistol, cocked it, and waved the boys away. They refused to move. The captain thrust his pistol into the side of the nearest lad and shouted loud enough to be heard yards away, *"Zurück."* The awaited shot did not sound; the boy, ragged and dirty, stared down the little officer, and in his own good time retrieved his bicycle and moved off lazily, teasingly, with his friends, to cheers from our side.

Similar scenes were being played out along the sector boundary. At Potsdamer Platz, the boundary was no longer the official one; for the day, a huge elongated pile of rubble became the substitute. It was ten to twenty feet high and edged by a sagging, bomb-torn brick wall. Along the top of the rubble, standing almost shoulder to shoulder, troops of the People's Army sweltered, some in rubber raincoats, others in tight green uniforms and high boots. A large crowd had gathered in the distance, while men and boys in the lee of the rubble wall heaved stones at the troops and yelled salty Berlin insults. It was a scene from an expressionist play of the 1920s: Georg Kaiser or Ernst Toller.

"Swine! You'd fire on your own workers! On your own mother!" One could smell that gunfire would break out.

"This is bad," a man near me said. *"Ganz schlimm."* A single shot cracked, and a man sat slowly down, both hands over his stomach. Vopo officers ranged up and down the line of troops, ordering them to maintain discipline.

I'd had enough. My notebook was full and my head empty. Walking along Ebertstrasse, I was joined by an east sector workman who said he was *"Arbeitslos"* (unemployed). He hooted at the Vopos as we went along, "Ja, you've got cigarettes to smoke. Enjoy them! Tonight we'll hang you from the lamp posts! By your dirty necks!"

Cravenly I cut loose from him; he was a clear target for the nearest itchy trigger finger. Images of the defiant boys stayed with me on my walk back to the Grunewald. Were they authentically brave, or was it that they lacked either the experience or the imagination to realize the possible consequences of their defiance? Or was it no more than *je m'en foutisme* Berlin style? Whatever it was, I was impressed.

The actions of the East Germans were another matter. Their example in Berlin promptly spread to the main cities of the DDR, resulting in chance deaths and purposeful execution of more than 200 people, so creating martyrs as well as hope among all Germans, and setting a pattern for opposition in the entire Soviet-occupied bloc. It became clear that neither Dibrowa, the military commandant in East Berlin, nor the Soviet military as a whole had been prepared, in 1953, to deal ruthlessly with the opposition, hence the bicycle boys in Berlin had been spared. The events of that year had put the fear of their atheistic gods in the Soviet leaders, so that by the time of the Hungarian uprising in 1956, in direct line from the DDR of 1953, the Soviets had learned a lesson: utter ruthlessness took the place of earlier temporizing. With hindsight it becomes apparent the Berlin *Aufstand* also led directly to the construction of *die Mauer,* the notorious wall, in 1960, and even more dramatically, to its destruction in 1989.

By the end of the 1953 academic year, I realized that I would have to return to the U.S. and to work paying a salary vaguely commensurate with my debts. An instructorship had been proposed in a state university. In a sense, Berlin had offered me a temporary refuge, as it had to the many transient refugees from Eastern Europe. Unlike them, I had profited from a trying year. I had gained some useful professional experience, and I had completed a book which at Salzburg I had been unable to touch. Preparing to leave, via England, I thought back to *Mitteleuropa,* to the serious fun of Salzburg, but mostly to my Berlin students; to their despair, barely held at bay in that blasted landscape; to their courage in the face of a problematic future; and to their childlike impression that history had come to a full stop in 1945. Now only the present, and a future no matter how chancy, had reality for them. I left believing that they were more fully victims of the preceding dreadful decades than they knew, but I honored them in ways that previously I would never have believed possible.

5

Return to Berlin

Leaving Berlin in 1953, I thought I was leaving for good, but in fall, 1954, I was back. This time I arrived with my very pregnant English wife, in a used and abused ex-British army van, bought with the advance for my first book. On my way back to America, as to an execution, I had paused in London again to meet the talented and beautiful woman whom I had interviewed two years before when travelling for the Salzburg Seminar. Stricken to pith and marrow, I renounced the return to my native land to try to exist by freelance writing and lecturing in London. An absentee divorce was arranged, and without sane prospects but optimistic as Candide, I proposed marriage and was accepted, to my immediate and continuing joy. While pleased to have a contract for my book, I was still piercingly aware that instead of resolving my financial troubles, I had compounded them.

A script for the BBC led to application for a job, but after having been short-listed, I was told that a work permit was impossible, and the post would have to go to a British subject. A lecture series for the London County Council was stopped for the same reason, and in the middle of a lecture on John Dos Pasos. It was too late to follow my American lead, even had I wanted to. What had I done to my lovely new wife? And to my ex-wife and to our son?

Despair was imminent, when Bogislav von Lindheim, professor of Anglo-Saxon in the Free University, Berlin, came to call on us in our London flat. Educated in England, a former tank commander on the

Russian front, Lindheim had been friendly to me in Berlin, a single exception to the chilliness of the rest of the senior German faculty. After some polite chat, he asked, "What would you think of returning to the Free University?"

I said the thought hadn't occurred to me; but I could not afford to go back as a temporary lecturer, if that was what he had in mind.

"That's not what I had in mind. The Philosophische Fakultät has voted to establish a chair in American Studies, and now the politicians have also approved. I took the liberty of proposing your name. Of course there would have to be a confirming vote, but I'm certain that will be no more than a formality."

I knew Lindheim to be as correct as he was tall and formal, not a man to come to London with vague gossip, and I felt a leap of un-tainted hope. Maybe there was a God after all. I told the sainted Lindheim yes, a professorship would interest me; he took his leave saying that he would put it all in writing as soon as possible.

Later I said to M that I had no doubts about why the chair had been offered to me, even though I hadn't published very much nor had a lot of teaching experience under my belt. American studies was not even my chosen field, comparative literature was, but I had written a disser-tation under the direction of Perry Miller, the most eminent American intellectual historian we had, whose recommendation carried weight. Few people in the field would leave green fields for life on a meager salary in a shattered, encircled city. As for the Germans, a chair in American studies would encourage American moral, political, and fi-nancial support, even though the appointee was untried and only po-tentially solid and established (qualities not then or ever pertaining to me).

M readily agreed to my decision to return to Berlin, although it would mean leaving behind family, friends, and the bright beginnings of a career in London as poet and novelist, for anonymity and mother-hood as Frau Professor McC. in Berlin. In my euphoria I apprehended her state only dimly, if at all, for the prospect of a reasonably decent life for M and our unborn child erased other considerations. M no doubt knew intuitively that life in Berlin would deprive her of the time, energy, and encouragement that was forthcoming in London, but she hid from me any reservations, never complaining during the five years we remained in Berlin, or thereafter, of the corkscrew turns that my career demanded of hers.

A year in London had made me aware of English ambiguity about postwar Germany. A residual dislike, bordering on hatred for the Germans, was unmistakable but understated, and accompanied among the educated by an ironic, traditional, and genuine admiration for German culture.[1] The same appeared to be the case among Americans, although without the irony. Many were of German descent, and memory of the wars was brief. Upon returning to Berlin, I observed the ambiguity among Germans themselves about that city.

Before 1870 and Bismarck's heavy-handed policy to try to unify the country, the long-established principalities had looked on Berlin as an ugly upstart, a self-presuming center of national life. Berliners were seen as Slavic interlopers, Prussian oppressors, military fops, and industrial johnnies-come-lately. After victory over France in 1870, German history turned apocalyptic, and Berlin became its center in fact, not in fancy. As citizens of the industrial, imperial, and military base of the country, Berliners' civic pride could turn into arrogance; only arrogance could account for its grotesque civic statuary and its grandiose architecture: an unfortunate mix of neo-classical, Assyrian, Egyptian, and hastily contrived fanciful. Not Bavaria, where National Socialism originated, but Berlin became the heart, liver and ganglia of the Nazi movement. In Hitler's plan, Berlin was to be reconceived, rebuilt, and renamed "Germania," the core of his thousand-year Reich, just as Rome had been the center of the Roman Empire. It was in Berlin that plans for the extermination camps became reality; from 1939–1945, the armies received their orders from Berlin; Berlin housed the infamous *Rassenamt*, the bureau devoted to racial purity, its banner "*Judenfrei* ."

Prophetically, Schopenhauer had called Berlin a "psychologically and morally cursed nest," while George Santayana's central character in *The Last Puritan*, Oliver Alden, remembers pre-1914 German "envy, hatred, and self-praise." We were to learn that the Soviets had tried to seal off Berlin in 1947, because the glitter of the western sectors, in contrast to the economic and industrial chaos of the east was a potential threat to Soviet hegemony. The western sectors of the city were a perpetual trade fair, in effect, in which capitalists flaunted luxury before the eyes of the impoverished east. It took fifty years for us to

---

1.   I use "culture" in its former sense, before it was hijacked by the anthropologists.

learn that between 1945 and 1948, Stalin dealt with the exposure of his armies to western delights by executing no fewer than 10,000 officers and men of the armies that had attacked and occupied Berlin.[2]

In Western Europe and in Western Germany, once-derogatory attitudes toward the city changed dramatically with the airlift of 1947–48 and the courage displayed by the Berliners. With plenty of Western media coverage, the citizens had indeed behaved admirably through a fraught time. Now they were portrayed as in the forefront of the cold war against the Soviet Union. Now the Berliners had justified their own views of themselves as tough, defiant, and spirited: the Londoners-under-the bombs of the continent. Unlike Londoners, however, as M and I came to learn, many in Berlin were given to self-pity and to an odd forgetfulness of the recent past. When we attended an early documentary film of the extermination camps, the first to be shown in Berlin, we sat among hundreds of people in the auditorium of the Free University in the most profound collective silence we had ever experienced.

That depiction of the dead and dying, together with the Berliners' popular image of themselves, brought to mind the experiences of the von Fritz family. Kurt and Louise von Fritz were foremost among people I had known (and envied) as exemplary in their courage and moral poise. She had been born into the Bavarian aristocracy, with close ties to the French; he had belonged to an aristocratic Prussian family. He was a classical scholar of solid achievement, and she an educated, charming, and lovely woman. Von Fritz was one of a small handful of German university professors who, as civil servants, had been required but had refused to take the oath of allegiance to the Nazis. Neither of the von Fritzes had Jewish blood; their decision to leave Germany was self-imposed. He was offered a place on the Columbia university faculty at once, and the family remained in New York City from the mid-1930s to 1948, when he joined the newly founded Free University.

Lindheim said that von Fritz was one of the few on the faculty who had bothered to read the reprints of the essays I had submitted as part of the appointment process, and that he had silenced any whisper of objection to my appointment. After Lindheim introduced us, we be-

---

2.   Alexandra Richie, *Faust's Metropolis: A History of Berlin* (London: Harper Collins, 1998), p. 616.

came warm, if formal, friends. M and I were asked to tea, where Louise greeted M, our two-month-old son in arms, with sympathy: "You poor young girl, alone in a strange land, a new baby to care for!"

M hinted that she did not feel quite like that, but I sensed that she was pleased at the sentiment.

"And what is the baby's name?"

"Peter Rufus, because of his red hair."

"I have a son named Peter, too," Louise said.

Slowly and deviously by way of common friends, we learned that Peter von Fritz had enlisted in the U.S. army and served in Europe after the invasion of Normandy. As lieutenant of infantry, he had led his platoon into one of the concentration camps, and not long afterward shot himself. It was impossible thereafter to refer to that event, but it accounted for Kurt's reticence and for Louise's constant and palpable sadness. Even her jokes were sad ones. When her mother lay dying in Bavaria, she told us, her Peter, then a little boy of four, hugged her and said, "Don't cry because Oma is dying, Mutti, because I'm going to be your Mutti now!" In New York, on the other hand, she said, when a neighbor's old mother died, two little grandchildren were bouncing on the sofa as Louise entered to offer her sympathy. "'Mrs. von Fritz, do you know how long it takes a body to rot in the grave? (Bounce, bounce went Louise on the sofa.) It takes four months!'" (Bounce, bounce) "And that is the difference between German children and American children," Louise concluded, amused.

Coming away from one of the frequent, four-hour-long faculty meetings late one fall afternoon, both of us reeking of the cigars neither of us smoked, I asked Kurt what it had been like to come back to Berlin after the war. He hesitated for a long time, a dozen paces, before answering, "Strange. It was so strange." He did not continue, and I did not press him. The same question arose spontaneously a few days later. M and I had been invited for drinks, and while Kurt prepared a tray in the kitchen, Louise told us that they had thought to "make things a bit easier" if they returned to their own language and familiar ways. By then we knew better than to ask what things.

"But did it?" M asked.

"Ah, no. People we had known in the past, acquaintances, friends, they seemed to see us as strangers. Worse, as deserters, traitors even. 'You got out of it, you went away,' they would say to us. 'Think of us. The bombs, hunger. We were robbed and raped when the Russians came.' They said these things and more. But never a word about the past, about those obscene camps."

Louise's complexity was compounded by her statelessness. When the von Fritzes left the United States to take up Kurt's post at the Free University, they had remained abroad beyond the time then prescribed for retaining their U.S. citizenship, thus they had unwittingly forfeited their American passports. Kurt applied for and received a German passport, but Louise, ashamed and at the same time outraged that she was supposed to apply for what by birthright was hers, remained imprisoned in her statelessness. She was scolded for her intransigence by another returned exile, as was Kurt for his indulgence of her position in the matter.

Over our Berlin years M and I would often visit them, but her sad gaiety and his absolute *Trauerigkeit* never left them. In faculty meetings, Kurt stood out by reason of the rational tenor of his comments, just as his American-English tweeds contrasted with the prevailing shabbiness of our cigar-smoking colleagues. Not long after we left Berlin in 1959, we learned of Louise's death. Kurt was to survive for several years, but we could not imagine his existence apart from that surprising, delightful woman.

Kurt and Louise von Fritz had found themselves returning from a foreign country in which they had been welcomed and honored, to an even more foreign native country, to hostility and isolation. The Jews who returned from abroad to Berlin in increasing numbers met a welcome similar to that of the gentile von Fritzes, yet subtly different. Of that number in the university, I had dealings only with K, a man whose attributes approached the grotesque. He had emigrated to a visiting lectureship in a good mid-western American university, a place, he announced, wanting in intellectual rigor, and unaware of the excellence his presence had conferred on the university. The American educational ethos was contemptible, and American students were retarded children. K did not converse, he lectured, and he lectured M and me in our own house about the shortcomings of American politics, the crudeness of our culture, and the sheer blindness of the U. of X for not promoting him to permanent rank.

K repeated his performance at many a dinner table, for colleagues went out of their way to be correct to K and his wife, but correctness had limits. A large, heavy man, K delighted in the endless faculty meetings, orating on any and all subjects. No one bothered to question his facts or to rise to his challenges; the assembled victims would scribble nonsense or stare at their shoes as he shouted platitudes in a piercing tenor. He was not loved, but over time I came to admire his pure, shining brass, his innocence of self-awareness.

The awful fact about K was that he seemed to all and sundry to embody a rabid anti-Semitic cliché; it was as though he had set out purposely to do so in order, perhaps, to test the post-Nazi climate of his native city. Although people were appalled by his manners, they allowed themselves to be cowed by his aggressiveness. By the time I left, K was no more admired than when he arrived, but he had built himself a firm power-base, trading on the residual, unspoken emotions that were entangled in the history of racial purity and wholesale death.

K was hardly representative of the increasing numbers of Jews who returned to take their proper place in the religious and civic life of the city. He came to seem no more than a bad joke in the face of an unspeakable history. Berlin had never established a ghetto; for that reason among others, the prewar Jewish population had been large, the numbers exaggerated in Nazi doctrine. Slowly and undramatically in the 1950s, Jewish institutions were reestablished: synagogues to replace those destroyed by the SS; an institute of Jewish Studies in the university; political representation in the City Council. Such attempts at restitution were fully supported by officials, and more to the point, by what I judged to be the population at large in West Berlin and in Western Germany. Nests of neo-Nazism and anti-Semitism remained in Bavaria and in certain other provinces; however, time proved them to be more annoying than effectual for forty years. Only with the resurgence of a quasi-Nazism in the 1990s among some young *Lumpenproletariat* (joined by some *Lumpenbourgeoisie),* a result of social and economic measures imposed upon the former communistic east, had we to be reminded of the unsavory past. Violence then was directed first at refugees and foreign-born workers, and for a change, only secondarily at Jewish cemeteries and synagogues.

Anna (Livia Plurabelle, of *Finnegans Wake*) my dachshund bitch, produced a son in London, to whom I also gave a Joycean name, "Bloom." Bloom arrived in Berlin as a puppy, to be made much of by passersby; Germans love dogs more than they love their mothers. Anonymous women encountered in the street would lecture us on Bloom's training and diet, and when we once tethered him outside the bakery on a length of rope, we were given hell for not providing so fine a dog with a proper leather lead. Always they would demand to know his name, and I would tell them "Bloom," at which they would at once address him as *"Bloomchen"* (little flower). I would inform them that Bloom was a Jewish dog, named for Leopold Bloom in Joyce's *Ulysses*. My stupid joke often touched a nerve and I would get a burning stare, silence, and the departure of the dog-lover. In my mind, "Bloom" and "Bloomchen" became a signature to the entire tortured history extending from *Kristallnacht* to the death camps to the airlift and the cold war. It still does.

Increasingly over the years in Berlin, M and I felt ourselves to be social spindrift, in but not of German society, nor of any integral part of either American or British official society. That feeling had not bothered me when I had lived alone in the city. With the birth of our son, Peter, our lives took on a new dimension with respect to nationality. Regarded as one of their own, M was welcomed in the British military hospital, which legally was regarded as British soil. Socially we continued to circulate only superficially among both Germans and occupiers, but now a subtle change became apparent. As for the Germans, both our cleaner from East Berlin and university people advised M to swaddle her infant, an idea of medieval horror to us. Invited to a wine-tasting evening, M asked someone's wife, also a recent mother, what she did about a sitter when she and her husband went out at night? The answer came with a laugh: "We do nothing. We just strap the baby in her crib."

"And if you go away for a weekend?"

"The same, except that we leave several bottles of milk in the crib."

I thought they might be pulling our legs, but they were not.

M soon found that she was unable to keep to her previous writing routine. The peculiarities of life in the encircled city did not help, nor, sad to say, my own preoccupation with my job and my writing.

All was not grim. At a dinner party given by the American cultural attaché, I argued with Gore Vidal about the alleged death of the novel, which he maintained had already occurred, and toward the end of the evening, I talked to the Irish wife of a French official. The lady had drunk copiously and demanded my card, which she thrust into the appealing aperture between her breasts, collapsed on the hall floor and managed to wrap herself in the oriental rug. Inured to her ways, her husband had departed earlier, instructing his chauffeur to return for Madame. The chauffeur picked up the Irish woman, rug and all, loaded her into the car and was off. I had to wonder what the French official would make of finding my card between his wife's breasts.

The encircled city was like good seats at an absorbing performance in a theater-in-the-round. The institute I directed had become a cultural outpost to the American cultural effort. Visitors would be sent to us: there was the eminent Japanese scientist whom we escorted in bitter January to an exhibit in East Berlin of paintings from Dresden. Instructed to take his passport with him, he carefully left it in his hotel. His face entirely hidden in a wool scarf, he sprinted like a startled pheasant past the Giorgiones, Tintorettos and Titians.

Kenneth Tynan, theater critic, knowing not a word of German, arrived with a request that we drive him to a performance in East Berlin of Bert Brecht's Theater am Schiffbauerdam. As I sat through my fifth visit to *Mutter Courage*, Tynan asked me *sotto voce* to translate for him. On his return to London, he produced an "authoritative" article on Brecht's total output and a critique of *Mutter Courage* in particular. I asked M if she had known Tynan at Oxford.

"Yes. But now he's so successful he has gone back to wearing ordinary clothes."

The mid-1950s were the golden years of the reptilian Senator Joseph McCarthy of Wisconsin, and of his even lower reptilian agents, Roy Cohn and David Schine, the unholy trinity whose mission was to cleanse the country of communism. Schine arrived in Berlin, to assure America that no communist books were being loaned to innocent Berliners by the American library, an offshoot of the State Department. The librarian, my good friend, was indignant when Schine went over her shelves, tossing out any titles that seemed to fill his peculiar bill. I had had an earlier encounter with Schine, when as senior tutor in the house he lived in at Harvard, I enjoyed the pleasure of drafting a letter to him to say that no, he could not keep his Cadillac on university property; and no, he could not conduct his father's hotel business with a female secretary in his rooms. Thanks to that young Savonarola's morning in the American library, my institute inherited the books he had found seditious, none of which had the slightest connection to communism by anyone's objective definition.

Against that background of high and low political intrigue, of cold war alarums and excursions, life went on in the serio-comic manner life had then and probably always has. M took our son, aged two, out in the newly fallen snow. She taught him to lie flat on his back, to extend his arms above his head and to move them up and down to create an angel. Delighted and giggling, he was making his third angel when a good Hausfrau approached, demanding to know what my wife thought she was doing. Did she not realize that the child must catch pneumonia? What sort of mother was she? In the spring, for contrast, when our Siamese cat, Albertine, disappeared for ten days, she was finally seen at the top of an eighty-foot tree near our flat. All the neighbors, German and British, turned out to debate how to lure Albertine down. The German fire brigade arrived with ladders but found then ten feet too short. Finally the baker's boy climbed the tree with a saw, and cut through the highest branch, on which Albertine perched. Meanwhile our neighbors, commanded by an RAF wing-commander, did a stately dance with a blanket extended for the rescue. Albertine coolly rode down on the severed branch, then six feet above the ground leapt off clear of the blanket and raced home, thin, hungry, dignity intact.

The more I thought about the incident, the more complex and irrational I found the whole philosophy of the occupation. Normally, military people and Berliners did not mix in any manner. Unspoken resentment on the part of the Berliners at what many saw as the unnecessary bombing of civilians was always present, but it came to the surface only in irony and jokes. The old Berlin Reithalle was now administered by the British: I had riding lessons from the German Reitmeister on superb horses for one mark an hour, but Germans were not permitted entry. When such uses and abuses came into question, the Allied response was, "Well, who started the war?" As time passed, more than ever I felt like a double agent: M and I as guests of Dietrich Fischer-Diskau, the only non-Germans present; the next day, tennis at the former German tennis club, no Germans allowed.

Work in the university went reasonably well. Two dozen degree candidates were studying with me, and my lectures were surprisingly well attended. I was now in, but not necessarily of, the German university system for life, if I so desired. A competent assistant coped with most of the administrative routine; a decent budget for books meant that our library was becoming respectable; the university calendar freed one from teaching for almost six months a year. As director of a European institute, I was even authorized to nominate people for the Nobel Prize in literature. Neither André Malraux nor Ernest Hemingway, my annual nominees, ever made it. Superficially I had little reason to regret having returned to Berlin, but complex regrets there were, existential rather than professional.

No one could ignore the steady flow of refugees from Stalinist Germany; their stories of deprivation and their hopes for a better life were constantly on our minds, in the press and in daily anecdote. What the Western press everywhere ignored was that large numbers of those refugees, disillusioned by what they found in the West, flowed back into the DDR. Try as we did, M and I could not ignore the sense of claustrophobia that life in the isolated city impressed upon us, in small but insistent ways. In free periods, we could hardly afford trips to England so that young Peter could get to know his grandparents and we could renew our ties there. Friendships in the diplomatic and military community were brief, for people were transferred constantly. Among Germans, the barrier of manners could not be circumvented. M and I would smile at a turn of phrase when our German friends showed consternation, and vice versa, thus rocking the social boat. Trying in our writing to hang on to our language, we would never become colloquially proficient in German.

When Peter turned four, we knew that we faced a major decision. He was learning good German in kindergarten, but my salary would never permit schooling abroad, even had we wanted that for him. If we remained in Berlin, our son would grow up with German loyalties and mannerisms; were we prepared for that? As we debated the issues, an offer from an American university arrived: to give me my present professorial rank and the means to organize a department of comparative literature. I so informed the dean of faculty, a charming ex-Jesuit, who promptly assured me that the Free University would equal the American offer and authorize me to establish an institute of comparative literature.

With many qualms as to what the dean and some colleagues might consider intellectual treachery, M and I determined to make the jump and to accept the American offer. Despite my strictures, I would leave behind several students and friends with whom we remained in touch over many decades. Berlin for M and me had been indelible in the record of our lives, and we were pleased to have witnessed that exciting, sad, and confusing episode in its history.

6

What Ivory Tower?

Men and women who teach in universities are often excoriated in the press and in other quarters for not doing enough to justify their rewards of a living salary, several weeks or months a year without having to be in the classroom, their research grants, and, for some, tenured positions. The craft or art or profession of teaching in an institution of higher learning is generally believed to house other-worldly types ensconced in an "ivory tower." I must confess that my own calling into that craft or art did not sound loud and clear; other horizons signaled invitingly: I could go back to sea; try to live by writing fiction and free-lance articles; become a newspaperman. Always my father's fate shrouded my mind, and feeling myself a coward for not risking the precarious, I chose the ivory tower. Once committed, I looked on those who had done little or nothing but read books by way of preparation with skepticism, if not hostility, only half-aware of my unfair snobbery, the snobbery of calloused hands. Colleagues to whom I responded most warmly were those who had worked with their hands, been to war, or otherwise brought to the classroom qualities generally believed to be foreign to pure scholarship.

In forty-some years in various universities, I had the good luck to make some good friends, and usually they were men who had come to university life in ambiguous or somehow unorthodox ways. Such thoughts were in my mind at the death of an unusually fine friend, Francis Fergusson, in December, 1986. He exemplified the qualities I admired as man, scholar, and writer, but the obituaries identified him merely as a professor and literary critic, which was like identifying Thomas Jefferson merely as a gentleman farmer. Born in 1904,

Fergusson's manners were those of a kinder day than ours. His reticence and unwillingness to thrust himself forward concealed versatility and mastery in several forms. By turns he was student of biology, of philosophy, writer, theater manager, occasional actor, playwright, poet, critic, university professor (meaning freedom to teach in any field he wished), husband, father of two, and stout friend. He belonged to his time and his country, and he found his time and his country worth belonging to. He was the most American literary man I ever knew, although never a flag-waver or spiritual cheer-leader. Once when I had just returned from a year in Europe, I complained to him that our president was illiterate, the congress a disgrace, and the voters insane. Francis replied, "I rather like all that."

His early upbringing shaped his character to an unusual degree. His father, Harvey B. Fergusson, had been born in Alabama in 1848; he attended Washington and Lee University, taught Greek and modern languages there, then became a lawyer. After practicing law in West Virginia, he went out to Albuquerque in the territory of New Mexico, where he staked out a claim to a silver mine. In 1887 he married Clara Hüning (1865–1950), who had been born in Albuquerque and educated partly in Germany. Harvey Fergusson became a delegate to the fifty-fifth Congress in 1897–99, a member of the Democratic National Committee during the Bryan campaign, and a member of Congress from 1911–15 (New Mexico having entered the Union in 1912).

On June 9, 1915, Harvey Fergusson was found hanging from the cottonwood tree in the courtyard of his residence in Albuquerque. Family accounts vary, but either the eleven-year-old Francis found the body or his mother did. Francis told his son, Harvey, that when his father's body was laid out for viewing, the throat had been cut from ear to ear. He had failed to be re-elected to Congress and had been acting strangely just before his death.

For a long time after that event, young Francis lost all appetite, subsisting for four years on the edge of starvation. By age fifteen he forced himself to eat a balanced diet, but the long deficiency left him with a slight spinal hump at shoulder level. A less obvious result of his father's suicide, I suspect, was his laconic cast, his reserve, together with his generosity and thoughtfulness to his own family and friends. At a further remove, the theatricality of his father's death might suggest his taste for theater, if not for his ensuing distinction in that activity.

M and I met Fergusson and his wife Marion at Bennington College, Vermont, in spring, 1957. After several years in Berlin I was beginning to dream in German; I was losing my grip on my own language, and both M and I agreed that a break, a year in the U.S., might be salutary for both of us. An exchange was arranged for the academic year 1956–57. Both Fergussons had been members of the founding faculty at Bennington, but in 1947 they left for Princeton. Now he was visiting Paul Feeley, prominent painter of the New York school, ex-Marine sergeant, marathon poker-player, and fly fisherman. Francis also fished, and visited Bennington each spring to work the Big Branch for trout. In our first meeting, he volunteered little, but he projected an authoritative presence. There was none of the customary "Where are you from?" that got on M's English nerves. (None of that either from the critic, Stanley Edgar Hyman, whose first words to us at Bennington were, "Finally my belly is bigger than my behind, so now my pants stay up." "How fascinating," M. answered.)

Later, I did not recall exactly what Francis had said, but I could not forget his full crop of gray hair or his facial expression, meditative and sad. Before we became colleagues in 1959, I had read all his writing, and over many a workday lunch or leisurely pre-dinner bourbon, he described episodes of his experience and showed aspects of his temperament that he kept from public view.

His American-ness derived in part from his roots in New Mexico, where he had learned Spanish as a small boy and observed the ways of the Hopi Indians. Two or three years after her husband's death, Clara Fergusson moved with Francis to Manhattan, where she made "pathetic" (Francis's word) attempts to increase her small income by decorating chinaware. Francis commuted to the Bronx High School of Science, then in 1920–21 attended the Ethical Culture School in Manhattan, where he formed life-long friendships with the writer, Jeannette Mirsky, and with Robert Oppenheimer, his exact contemporary. Francis entered Harvard in 1921, and Oppenheimer followed a year later, delayed by illness. At Harvard, Francis studied biology, partly because of Oppenheimer's influence, but he was already reading Dante, philosophy, writing verse, and a novel that has not survived. During the holidays he visited Oppenheimer's parents in New York, and went back to New Mexico for the summers.

Harvard gave him a partial scholarship, and after his second year, he won a Rhodes Scholarship to Queen's College, Oxford. A very young man's iconoclasm dominates a letter to his old friend, Paul Horgan, in New Mexico. Written aboard the Cunarder RMS *Albania,* the letter describes his fellow Rhodes Scholars as "morons. . . . they're as easy to find anything in common with as so many dolphins. The southerners smoke cigars and play poker; an aesthete reads art history, others on investigation prove 'pretty low.'" After a year of loneliness in which he worked in biology with the great Sherrington, he found he hadn't enough mathematics to go on, and shifted to Modern Greats (politics, philosophy, and economics). In the summers of 1924 and 1925 he took part in the "Entretiens de Pontigny," which were attended by such as Mauriac, Martin duGard, Malraux, Maurois, Gide, Valéry, Schlumberger, Aron, Ramón Fernandez, Robert Curtius, and even Lytton Strachey. In addition to widening his perspectives in many ways, Pontigny probably provided him the model for the Princeton seminars in literary criticism, of which he became the first director in 1949. At some station along the Oxford way, Fergusson's isolation ceased. He joined the poetry society and became gregarious. "He knows everyone at Oxford," Oppenheimer wrote, "he goes to tea with Lady Ottoline Morrell, the high priestess of civilized society, & the patroness of Eliot and Berty [Russell]." In that company, Oppenheimer added, "he learned how to treat dukes."

Fergusson and Oppenheimer had been reunited in England; Oppenheimer was working at Cambridge University, and the two spent the Christmas holidays of 1925–26 in Paris. It is no secret that for all his brilliance, Oppenheimer was given to alarming psychotic episodes. In the course of one of their discussions in Paris, Oppenheimer came up on Francis from behind, and in earnest or in jest, tried to throttle him. After a tussle, Francis emerged unscathed but concerned. On his return to Cambridge, Oppenheimer apologized by letter, and Francis did his utmost to stand by his friend in later episodes of depression and despair that not even a Harley Street psychiatrist could alleviate.

With a second-class honours degree, Fergusson returned to the United States in late summer, 1926. A performance by the Old Vic company in 1925, he told his son, Harvey, determined him to spend his life in the theater. He settled in Manhattan and began four years of work in the American Laboratory Theatre, where he learned the techniques of the Moscow Art Theatre, and met Marion Crowne, whom he married in 1931.The Laboratory Theatre was directed by Richard Boleslavsky and Maria Ouspenskaya, protegées of Stanislavsky. His insistence on the necessity of an integrated repertory company, on a mix of classical and modern work, and on full intellectual and physical involvement of the actors gave Fergusson a basis for his own work in the theater and for aspects of his work on Dante and Shakespeare.

As Boleslavsky's theater director, Fergusson was plunged at once into the leading and most enduring tradition of the modern theater movement in Europe and the United States, and he was forced to learn every large and small aspect of theatrical production. As early as December, 1927, Francis had found his first and enduring principle, fidelity to the text, bucking Boleslavsky himself over textual changes in *Much Ado About Nothing* that the master had wanted. Not everything was theater. He saw Oppenheimer from time to time, and was reading Dante on the side. The apprentice years mattered considerably in Fergusson's career, for while his later life was given over mainly to teaching and writing, he remained first an artist in his approach to his later work. His range, from the Greeks to Pirandello to Scott Fitzgerald and beyond, was the range of an accomplished actor, but one whose writings on the moderns reflected tradition, and the terms and disciplines of the past.

The depression meant the end of the Laboratory Theatre, and for Fergusson a forced turn to drama criticism, to writing for and editing *Hound and Horn,* an excellent literary journal while it lasted (to 1934), when he moved on to lecturing on drama and literature at the New School for Social Research. He once wrote that Moliére acquired "his extraordinary mastery of the stage itself, in the only way, the hard way." Fergusson wrote that with authority, for his knowledge was acquired exactly like Moliére's. He and his wife spent thirteen years from 1934 as members of the faculty at Bennington College, where he directed the theater and lectured on literature; his wife taught acting. In those years Fergusson was able to integrate his various approaches to the past into a theory of what could be, of what is or is not possible on a stage, and how best to explain to himself, to his students, and to the world a theory of art adapted from all his previous practical and theoretical work.

Fergusson said to an interviewer in 1972 that at Bennington he continued to use the methods of the Laboratory Theatre, "not only in directing plays, but in the analysis of the poetry, fiction and drama which I continued to teach in the literature division. I still use [them] whenever I work on literature; I think the Moscow Art Theatre's notion of 'action' is essentially the same as Aristotle's, and that Aristotle's theory of drama and other arts as 'the imitation of an action' is much the best we have." Throughout Fergusson's career, he continued to meditate on, to apply, and to enlarge that Aristotelian term, which in the *Poetics* most readers find at once seductive and ambiguous.

In his introduction to *The Idea of a Theater,* Fergusson compared the Elizabethan theater, "which had been formed at the center of the culture of its time," with the modern period, in which "human nature seems to us a hopelessly elusive and uncandid entity," creating impossible conditions for the contemporary playwright. Aristotelian action accordingly, became equally elusive. In an essay of 1932, Fergusson compared Ibsen's work with James Joyce's *Exiles.* In Ibsen he found the purest modern equivalent of Aristotelian action. Ibsen's characters are still representative, they still reflect a unifying thesis deriving from ethical impulse, while Joyce "substitutes for action a motionless picture, and for a thesis a metaphysical vision of a kind of godless monadology or Pluralistic Universe, of a consistency and strictness which William James the liberal never dreamed of." In another context, Fergusson compared Henry James and Chekhov, discovering the use of social ceremony in Chekhov akin to that of Henry James, their purposes identical: "to focus attention on an action which all share by analogy, instead of upon the reasoned purpose of any individual, as Ibsen does in his drama of ethical motivation."

The contemporary theater in New York had sold out, Fergusson believed. He wrote that "each poetic dramatist platonically discerns his own beautiful, consistent and intelligible dramatic idea while the formless population, looking the other way, is engrossed in the commercially profitable shadows on the cave wall." His own ability as a playwright is evident in *Penelope,* a version of Odysseus's return to Ithaca. His opinion of the New York theater was not enhanced by the commercial failure of his musical verse-play, *The King and the Duke* (mid-1930s, after the episode in *Huckleberry Finn*), produced at the Circle-in the Square in 1953. By 1957 he could be impolite, for him, about it all, referring to the New York theater as "the schizophrenic Eden of the middle-brows, where everyone is nice *and* rich."

Thus the artist continued to predominate over the lecturer. The second of Fergusson's formative ideas, one allied to his idea of action, is his use of the term "tragic rhythm." Always meticulous in acknowledging his sources, he noted that Scott Buchanan had found tragic rhythm to have been taken over by natural science, a statement of Fergusson's own naturalism, as I read it, and a source of his cheerful pessimism. (Trouble would be greeted with a Yiddish "oi yoi," a Spanish "Aiee," or a simple German "Himmel.") By moving from biology to theater, Fergusson had tried in one sense to deny the truth he recognized in the insight of the mathematician, Buchanan, concerning modern society. The whole attempt suggests the unity of Fergusson's mind and career, in which tragic rhythm informs his life and thought.

Fergusson left Bennington at the end of 1947 to spend two years at the Institute for Advanced Study in Princeton, at the invitation of Oppenheimer, the director. There he wrote *The Idea of a Theater*, the book that earned his international reputation. As noted, from 1949–1952 he was the founding director of the Princeton Seminars in Criticism (re-named the Christian Gauss Seminars in Literary Criticism in 1952). He also taught in the English division of the modern language department. After a year at the University of Indiana, he was named University Professor at Rutgers, remaining there until his retirement in 1969.

The course of Fergusson's life in American universities was not smooth. Having only a mere Oxford M.A. but no validating American Ph.D., he was regarded in some quarters as unqualified to breathe the thin, Castalian air of the tenured professoriat. Although his university professorship meant that he outranked full professors, established departments at Rutgers refused him hospitality, until the German department offered an office in what he called "a broom closet." When I arrived in 1959, it was in his broom closet, wryly amused, that I found him. By 1961, he was my senior and honored colleague in the newly founded graduate department of comparative literature, where he occupied a suitable office in our headquarters. There his influence on all, faculty and students alike, was subtle and pervasive. His standards, we hoped, would be our standards, and his bearing affected even the most unkempt lout among his students. He was generous with his personal attention to students, taking time, as the novelist and critic, Alan Cheuse later put it, "to read my awful undergraduate stories, telling me that my language 'showed promise.'" After Francis's death, the poet Robert Pinsky said that as he was lecturing at Berkeley, "I heard Francis *speaking through* me." Even as he taught undergraduates and advised graduates, Francis indicated skepticism about the Ph.D. mills in which he was a miller, an attitude that made for health and candor in our offerings, I like to believe.

To the American followers of the Barthes-Foucault-Derrida school, and to specialists in what they arrogantly call "theory," Fergusson's work looks old fashioned, as indeed it might in his fidelity to tradition and to historical knowledge. But as the best writing always does, his stands outside and beyond fashion. Unlike Richard Blackmur, whose temperament was similar to Fergusson's, Francis wrote prose that is limpid and quotable, where Blackmur's prose is obscure, thick with qualification. In his early essay on Joyce, Fergusson wrote, "Nowhere outside *Exiles* will you find human isolation so finely rendered—that obstinate incommensurability of human longings which seems to be the cold little wisdom of our time. . . ." Thirty-four years later he wrote that "the critic must learn to spend his little energies where they will do the most good, distinguishing what is essential in literature from what is accidental, peripheral, trivial, or merely temporary." In two words he compressed familiarity and judgment by describing as "complacent provinciality" Voltaire's preference for his own version of Oedipus over that of Sophocles. In another vein, Fergusson found Molière's comedy akin "to the modest sweetness of seventeenth-century music."

Fergusson's style is prominently American, an example of the American plain style, free from what Allen Tate called "scholarly rubbish." The diction can be surprising, as when he used slang and colloquialism: he wrote that Molière's theater "has that alert and worldly pep which is properly called the *esprit gaulois.* " "Pep," a word from the 1920s and George Babbitt's favorite, is thus resuscitated and given currency. An American barb lodges in Fergusson's description of Kenneth Burke's style as a "perpetual-motion machine, or jungle gym for exercising and deflating the literary mind."

In 1954, Francis bought a frame house on five acres of land on a quiet road in the outskirts of Kingston, New Jersey, three miles from Princeton. His acreage sloped down from the road to a swamp, and the land had become jungle. Patiently he cleared the undergrowth, selectively felled trees, and over the years created a handsome garden. Drama continued to preoccupy him: he saw Dante's epic poem as drama, and through his theories of action and tragic rhythm, he found ways of comparing Dante and Shakespeare. Ibsen and Pirandello regularly appeared on his course lists, while he ranged up and down European and American literature in his courses for undergraduates. His writing during these years was not voluminous, but it was steady and valuable. *Dante's Drama of the Mind* appeared in 1953, followed by *The Human Image in Dramatic Literature: Essays* in 1957; *Poems 1929–1961* in 1962; *Dante* in1966; *Shakespeare, The Pattern in His Carpet,* 1970; *Literary Landmarks* ,1975 ; and *Trope and Allegory,* 1977. Honors accrued as he aged, and with them came invitations and travels: to Japan, to Somalia for a visit to his son in the U.S. consulate; to Italy, Puerto Rico, Hawaii, Spain.

Marion Fergusson had died in 1959. Three years later, after a period of bleak solitude, Francis married Peggy Kaiser, a widowed Englishwoman and friend from Bennington days. A gifted painter and a zealous gardener, Peggy devoted herself to Francis and made their house a delight to visit in all seasons. Francis was never more content than when sitting in his garden in summer, or at his kitchen window at dusk in winter, to watch deer browsing on the land, or rabbits, and more than once, a vixen and her cubs at play.

After his retirement from teaching, friends urged him to write an autobiography, or at least a memoir about his early days in New Mexico: rafting on the Rio Grande with his elder brother; concealing themselves to watch a secret Hopi ritual. I knew that Francis was too self-effacing to write about himself. He proposed instead to write about his friends, a project that involved long research and copious notes about Robert Oppenheimer. That nuclear scientist's misadventures in Washington, D.C. elicited Francis's loyalty and his resolution to put right what he believed to be others' poor efforts to present his friend to a wide public. At the same time he saw a good deal of other friends, not because they were eminent, but because they were friends: Richard Blackmur, Roger Sessions, Allen Tate. By chance, the Fergussons were visiting the Oppenheimers on the night of Robert's death in February, 1967.

Francis's work on Oppenheimer came to an end, gradually but inevitably as Parkinson's disease invaded his body. Never a man to complain, he seemed to become serene and even cheerful as the disease slowly crippled him. His legs began to fail him, but even when it was agony for a visitor to see him walk, he would insist on pulling up a chair for a woman, and would himself prepare the visitors' drinks. During his final five years, he not only became immobile, but his ability to swallow was diminished; he could speak only slowly and

with difficulty. Yet on one occasion when my wife briefly relieved
Peggy from her nursing cares, Francis failed to begin his lunch, and
when my wife questioned him, he replied "I was waiting for you to
begin." In hospital at low periods, pale and gaunt, he became a favorite of the nurses, always finding strength to ask how *they* were feeling.

Years before, when I had been reading his book on Dante, I asked
Francis whether he had been exposed to any sort of religious training,
because I found his grasp of Dante's theology to be that not only of a
scholar but of a scholar-believer. "Oh, no," he answered. "I've always
been an atheist." He added that his father had been an atheist, as was
his father's father and mother and her father. I recalled that when
Peggy told me that during Francis's final stay in hospital, a clergyman
turned up in his room to ask, "Have you thought about God?" Francis,
who had not spoken for days, replied "I don't believe in God." "But
God believes in you," the clergyman insisted, at which Francis rolled
his eyes upward toward Peggy, and the clergyman mercifully went
away.

I remember Francis in hospital, sitting in a wheelchair and looking
out on the public street, believing that he was in his kitchen, watching
the deer. With that memory came to mind the beautiful short story of
J.F. Powers, "Lions, Harts, Leaping Does," which I had read years
before. It concerns an aged Franciscan priest, Father Didymus, who in
winter, like Francis Fergusson at this time, is near death. A lay brother,
Titus, is devoted to him, and to pass the time reads to him from the
lives of the saints, particularly those accused of heresy, Didymus's
favorites. As death approaches, he asks Titus to read "Lions, Harts,
Leaping Does," a title that he has imagined, just as Francis had imagined the deer he saw in Witherspoon Street, Princeton, through the
hospital window.

At Francis's death in the week before Christmas, I remembered his
poem, "A Suite for Winter," in which he seemed to have anticipated,
and by anticipating, to have transcended, his own death. The final
stanzas read:

When the year moves toward cold and dark, the city
    denies with its myriad glitter of light
    the primitive chill of terror and pity

Which is the signal of the coming night
    of winter. Curled within its cozy fringe
    of fur, the mindless creature can sleep tight;

But the waking spirit feels the cold impinge
    upon the hidden quick of its desire,
    night edge its little vision with the tinge

Of boundless dark. What then would it require
    to make those gentle faces disappear,
    sparks in the black abyss like this brief fire,
    Christmas lights that come with the cold of the year?

Many may hear Francis Fergusson speaking through them, but he was
a man unlikely to have exact sequel or analogue.

7

In Defense of Poesie and Bullfighting

Life in the ivory tower, with its jealousies, cabals, and intrigues over parking spaces can become tedious, but it may also contain surprises. After a tantalizing taste of Malaga in 1936 and a subsequent taste for Spain, its language and its ways, the academy enabled me to return by a devious path to Spain and to that unique and theatrical art, *toreo,* the only proper word for bullfighting.

Let us leap ahead to Madrid in the 1990s and to the feast of San Isidro. In Goya's time that fiesta occupied a weekend at most, but for commercial reasons of late, it has been extended to two weeks, then three, then a full month. For many Madrileños, San Isidro is dominated by daily *corridos de toros* (bullfights), but for me, the corridas in late afternoon meant mornings free for the Prado and its glorious pictures. On the morning of May 15, 19—the approach to the museum along the Paseo del Prado had been washed down and smelled of grass and spring flowers, despite the car exhausts from the road alongside. In the queue at the entrance, a man behind me struck up a conversation to pass the time. He proved to be an Irish missionary who, after twenty-nine years in Nigeria, was in Madrid for the first time, having stopped off on his way to Dublin. "And what brings you here?" he asked.

I said that I had come as often as possible over the years for the *corridas* of San Isidro, the fiesta that Goya had depicted in paint and in the cartoons for tapestries in the Royal Palace.

"Ah yes. Isidore. I looked him up yesterday in the register. It seems that if he existed at all, he was most probably a minor pagan god."

It struck me that in the years of Franco and even before, the notion of the patron saint of Madrid as a pagan god would have been unsettling if not heretical on the lips of a priest, but now the idea of a pagan Isidore would unsettle no one. Isidore, or Fortuna, had eased the steady transition of Spain from a police state to a constitutional monarchy, with only the operatic moves of a bunch of colonels in February, 1981, to challenge that transition. Spain and especially Madrid was now open where it had been closed, candid where it had been secretive, and eager where it had been reluctant. Even so, foreign commentators tend to take Spain now at face value, as a country that has shed its dubious past: priest-ridden, dirty, cruel, and barbarous, to join happily the three-piece-suited world of easy cash and hard consumption.

The streets of old Madrid, formerly austere, beautiful, and run-down, had dumpsters laden with fragments of seventeenth-century oaken paneling, plaster and assorted litter, all to make way for new construction. New cars creep through their own smog; on cold days the entire population wears costly black leather. Mere economic analysis, the melodrama of the stock market, and the resemblance of parts of Madrid to a dozen other cities dominated by banks, office buildings, air pollution and drugs fails to reveal redeeming continuities in the social texture of Spain. At the most superficial level, I noted that while the old woman sitting in the sun in the park outside the opera was wearing a sweatshirt inscribed "Las Vegas" rather than the traditional black of mourning, the same sad, often beautiful face of the past, of a hundred paintings, contrasted to her painfully contemporary costume. In the subway to Las Ventas, the *plaza de toros,* not all was black leather. With the hot weather, many men removed their socks and endured the heat in winter-weight shoes. Modernity had not triumphed for the man who had to slap his wrist to make his digital watch register the time.

Such impressions reinforced a long-held conviction that to come to terms with the Spanish temperament in all its manifestations, one cannot ignore the place of *toreo* in Spanish society. Even (or particularly) good Hispanists back in the ivory tower get things wrong by subscribing to the stereotype in Western society of *toreo* as a bloodthirsty throwback, at best a casual diversion of a perverted, savage place. *Toreo* is anything but a casual diversion. It has figured significantly in the history of the Catholic Church in Spain, in civil and criminal law, in the divisions in society by class, in the language, in the arts, and for better or worse, in the politics, manners and mores of generations.

Cultural anthropologists such as Julio Caro Baroja and Julian Pitt-Rivers, and the folklorist, A. Alvarez de Miranda, find the cult of the bull as a sacred object and as savage beast at archeological sites in many parts of the world. They insist that the cult has endured in Spain and lies deep in the folk memory.

Mystical speculation about ancient, sacred bull-rites apart, it is certain that Catholicism and *toreo* have been intimately connected for more than two centuries. With the development of *toreo a pie*[1] created the prospect of death on the horns of a bull, a prospect that could not fail to make the comforts of Catholicism completely beguiling. Previously the lancing of bulls on horseback had been a diversion for aristocrats. Now mere commoners developed first the craft, then the art of controlling a fierce animal with capes and killing it with a sword. With the appearance of the professional matador (literally "killer"), who contemplates his fate daily, genuine faith, superstition, or both led to a special reliance on the blessings and intercessions of the Church.

Spain remains not only nominally but actually Catholic; even men now go to church. *Corridas* are still celebrated on the saint's day of village, town, or city. Often in the past and continuing in outlying districts into the present, priests were expected to *torear*[2] in the village plaza on the saint's day. In the nineteenth century, the Vatican threatened excommunication for such activity. In Andalusia the Carthusians, Augustinians, and Dominicans operated for profit *ganaderías* (breeding ranches) of *toros bravos* (fighting bulls; also called *toros de lidia*[3]). Some have suggested that the sacrifice of the mass and the sacrifice of the bull derive from a common religious ancestor.

Toreo has been involved in politics often, and often deplorably, as when Generalissimo Franco tried to take over the entire profession with some success by improving conditions and raising pensions. In 1898, year of doom for the Spanish empire, Juan López Valdemoro, Conde de las Navas, published *El espectáculo más nacional*, his attempt to revive Spanish pride with an impassioned, nationalistic ex-

---

1. Bullfighting on foot, as opposed to *rejoneo*, in which a rider on horseback attempts to work and to kill the bull on horseback.
2. Totally untranslateable. It means to work, or play the animal in such a manner as to prepare it for an immediate and efficient death by sword. No one can "fight" a bull as our English absurdity has it. *Torear* is an infinitive, hence the preposition "to" is also absurd.
3. Cf. note 10. *Lidiar = torear*.

amination of *toreo*. "We have slept under our laurels for too many years without looking beyond our borders. We may not be so tremendously patriotic as the English, so artistic as the Italians, so powerful as the Russians, so industrial and elegant as the French, . . . nor so peaceful as the Swiss, but let us not be ashamed to be *toreros,* for . . . in our national spectacle *there is plenty of iron* [sic] with which to cure our anaemia."

In politics, *toreo* traditionally has been associated with the Spanish right wing. It was the aristocratic landowners who had the land on which to breed *toros de lidia* as an avocation as much as for profit. At the same time the Spanish conception of chivalry, with its emphasis on personal honor and duty, was transmitted to the profession of *toreo* and remains predominant. Every first-class plaza has a royal box, often occupied by royalty. The left wing in Spain and elsewhere has always seen *toreo* as circuses, if not bread, a sop to the oppressed masses.

As to language, *toreo* has figured in a great deal of writing, good and bad. In everyday speech, the Spanish are inventive but not literary. *Toreo* has spawned an entire language and sub-language, often obscene, always comic, the tang of which can carry over into polite speech. If the Madrid public finds a bull too small, or crippled, but still being worked by a highly paid matador, entire tiers of the plaza show their displeasure by meowing en masse.

If *toreo* is not a brutal anachronism, what is it? And how can good scholars ignore its place in the scheme of things? Briefly put, *toreo* is not the savage mess that many tourists pronounce it to be, but an art form requiring study, taste, observation, and a measure of dedication and patience, like any other art, before its essence and aesthetic quality emerge. To the confirmed aficionado, at its all-too rare best *toreo* combines the torero's[4] training, experience, intuition, control, craft, imagination, and spontaneity. It does not depend upon agility or athletic ability alone, but it demands immediate recognition of each animal's possibilities and the almost instant devising of a plan for dispatching it with grace and authority, according to the canons of the craft and art. For these and many other reasons, *toreo* as an art form is unique in that the *torero* cannot commit errors without grievous risk;

---

4.   The word defines all who face the *toro* : matador, picador, *banderilleros*.

he cannot paint over a mistake or rewrite a paragraph. It is not a pure art but a mixed one; it is an art of performance, like ballet, and like opera and theater, it demands the complicity of many and varied people for its existence.

Almost everyone not resident in Spain, Mexico, or a handful of South American countries would deny the status of art to an activity they see only as a cruel sport. The Spanish application to the European Economic Community was delayed for years, in part because of "bull-fighting," and in 1988 several members of the Council of Europe proposed a resolution requiring Spain to abolish the practice. Such gestures, deriving from low politics and high-mindedness, are fortified in the efforts of Greenpeace, Animal Rights, Save the Elephants, and related admirable and idealistic ventures. To the charge of cruelty, one answer is that the *toro* is bred to die a glorious death in the plaza. Another answer is yes, it is cruel, but that such public cruelty reflects the cruelty of the animal world in nature.

The charge of cruelty must involve one conception of tragedy, a distinctly Spanish one. I find that the faces of Spaniards everywhere are the same faces one sees in the Spanish galleries of the Prado and other collections: inward-looking, never really vapid, often indeed tragic in Unamuno's sense of the word. In his book *Del sentimiento trágico de la vida* he writes of the "war" between rational skepticism and the human urge to faith in immortality. The tragic sense of life accommodates cruelty, just as troops in combat accommodate, in some manner, the deaths of comrades. True, the inept and splashy killings of bulls one sees all too often are cruel, but cruel for reasons not immediately apparent to most spectators. Such cruelty results from unscrupulous managers who pick up a raw, talented boy and arrange for him to take on bulls he cannot cope with for lack of full training and experience. Other cruelties result from impresarios and veterinarians who permit the animals' horns to be sawed and filed, thus throwing off their timing; from breeders who sell bulls that formerly they would have rejected; and from venal critics who take bribes to praise indifferent or abysmal performances.

Toreo distinctly is not a sport, not a contest between man and animal. The bull must die, in public, even if it has wounded or killed the matador opposing it; in which case the surviving senior matador must finish off that animal. The outcome of each segment of the *corrida* is known in advance, and the *torero's* every motion, if he is any good, contributes in its set order to the bull's death. No one bets on *corridas,* as on sports, nor do Spanish children go about in matador's garb casually, as our children wear baseball caps to bed and dress in quarterbacks' jerseys. *Toreo* is profound as sport never pretends to be, serious in a way that a Mickey Moused culture is unprepared for. Further, *toreo* may be considered as art in that a vivid and necessary relationship exists between what occurs in the plaza and assessment by an informed, independent body of critics.

The Civil War of 1936–39 devastated not only all Spain, but *toreo* as well. Herds were slaughtered for meat, while Franco's subsequent police state caused standards in many of aspects of life to degenerate, *toreo* not least. Underage bulls, inflated and venal criticism, blind eyes to abuses: all conspired to decadence. Reforms began with Franco's death in 1975 and the emergence of democratic forms coincided with a regained respect and enforcement of the official regulations of every aspect of *toreo.* By the late 1980s, prosperity encouraged a formerly small, depressed middle class to become a large, spirited group, dominated by the young with pesetas to spare. A new public crowded into the plazas as never before, a change from the half-empty plazas of the early seventies. No two people agree fully on reasons for the change, but the most thoughtful Madrileños relate memories of an agricultural nation fast turning suburban, and efforts to remain in touch with realities of the past to be found now in the *plaza de toros.* For whatever reason, *toreo* had become fashionable; books on the subject abounded, and a new, ignorant public had available in the press a learned and intelligent body of criticism unseen for generations.

Not all is well with Spain or its national art-spectacle. Inflation has wrought great harm, to the degree that the ordinary spectator of the past, the working class and the poor, who were among the most faithful and knowledgeable of aficionados, could not afford the high ticket prices. The best places now go to company executives and their guests, who know little and care less about what they are seeing, but to whom it matters to be seen. Scarcity of good bulls means that inferior animals are passed by the veterinarians, while the finest bulls often are sold to France, where ticket-prices are even higher than in Spain. The integrity of *toreo* is again endangered, but like opera, theater, poetry, the novel, music composition, *toreo* staggers from crisis to crisis but manages in some fashion to survive. Its best hope lies in the many schools that train aspiring *toreros* well, in the few, newly excellent newspapers that print exacting criticism, and in the many periodicals and books on the subject at last available.

Any slight authority for the foregoing derives from a remote past. In early winter, 1961, I found myself in the smaller of the two plazas of Mexico City, El Toreo, chatting with two established Mexican matadors while resting on the *estribo* (interior foot rail) of the plaza after a stint of training under the hot winter sun. My daily function was mainly to run a pair of horns mounted on a billet of wood, in order to simulate the charge of a *toro de lidia* for the professionals, while trying to learn from them the mental and physical techniques of their work. When the matadors had had enough, I would go to work with my own cape, muleta, and sword at the charge of an imaginary bull, or horns run by other aspiring *toreros*. My efforts were subject to constant criticism by Mario Sevilla, a retired Mexican matador. At age forty-three I had no illusions about becoming anything more than conversant with the art of *toreo*. My first motive was to enter the enclosed ambience of that art-spectacle-business in order to write a book in English that would put straight what I considered to be misapprehensions fostered by Ernest Hemingway in his first novel, *The Sun Also Rises,* most fully in *Death in the Afternoon,* in several short stories, and in his taurine journalism. *Death in the Afternoon* had not been translated into Spanish in 1961, so I asked the matadors, never noted as a group for wide reading, if they knew Hemingway's book, which I translated literally as "Muerte en la tarde." They laughed, and Manolo said, "Look here, a man doesn't go into the plaza to die. We go to the bulls to *live.* " I at once recognized that he meant by that " to live" in the fullest sense that life offers, not just to subsist.

Hemingway was partly to blame, I believed, for the widespread notion that Spain and its former colonies were barbarous, while his emphasis on blood and guts, death inevitable, violates the matadors' belief that a man caught by the bull is not a hero, but inept. He has failed to know his bull and failed to observe the canons of his art that had evolved in order to demonstrate the recourses to avoid disaster. Overtones of tragedy are present in the finest *corridas,* but not for Hemingway's reasons. He chose to glorify the *torero,* but from the purist's point of view, he all but ignored the primary place of the *toro.* Respectable criticism of a *corrida* inevitably includes an assessment of the animals, their provenance, age, weight, horns, and general condition. Hemingway knew all that, but writing for a mass readership, he deleted such matters in the main, just as he invented a great deal of cheap melodrama in the travesty written for *Life* magazine and published as *The Dangerous Summer.*

I had seen my first *corrida* in Maracay, Venezuela, in 1936. Both the bulls and the only memorable matador on that occasion were Mexican. Luis Castro, "El Soldado," stayed in the mind for his nonchalance, an unhurried mastery, which I lacked the knowledge to analyze, and for his unsmiling and purposeful failure to play up to the spectators: no hotdogging, but pure, classical technique. What with earning a living and service in World War II, I saw no more *corridas* until after the war, but the memory of Luis Castro never faded. I did manage to collect books on *toreo,* and with them impatience at the decayed romanticism and the inflated prose of so many of them festered.

An invitation to teach in the National University in Mexico City led to an introduction to Mario Sevilla, who wanted to write a book on *toreo.* I told Sevilla that I despaired of books in English on the subject, and that I hadn't found Spanish books much better. I had wanted to write a book on *toreo* for a long time, but I could never know enough about it to do the job properly. Finally we agreed to write jointly the book the world was crying out for. Mario said, "If you are serious, you have to learn the fundamentals. You can't just think about them."

"Fine. You teach me."

The next fourteen months were exhilarating, exhausting, and more informative than I had believed possible. My seminar in comparative literary criticism at the university took place in the late afternoons, three days a week. On five or six days a week, I would rise at 5:30, drive to Mario's by six, rouse him from his bed, and make for Chapultepec Park, where among early walkers and practitioners of yoga I could learn the rudiments of the cape and *muleta* (small cape mounted on a wooden handle) in the semi-privacy of that urban forest. Mario, then in his late fifties and pudgy, would lecture, reminisce, and answer my questions, pausing to reprimand me for a tendency to *codear,* or hold my elbows close to my body. Dangerous, for safety lies in keeping the still imaginary bull at arm's length. "'Extend your arms and *torear* as though you had no body,'" he would say, quoting the great matador, Domingo Ortega; or he'd shout, *"muñeca, muñeca "* (wrist), impressing on me the technique of aligning passes with the *muleta* by bringing the animal around with both arm-movement and a full turn of the wrist.

An early lesson at Chapultepec came not from Mario but from an adolescent passerby. He was accustomed to seeing youngsters like himself passing imaginary bulls, but a man of my age was unthinkable. "Who is this señor?" he asked Mario.

"Ask the señor. He speaks Castilian." When he asked my name, I suppressed an impulse to tell him to go climb a tree, but told him my name anyway. This was his country, not mine.

"What kind of name is that?"

"It's Irish."

The intruder considered that, as I continued trying to perfect a left-handed pass, the *natural*, and still look natural. Finally he asked, "What is your mother's name?"

"Her name was Beauchemin."

"Una francesa?"

"Si."

He smiled in relief. A French mother explained how a gringo could have the *sangre,* the necessary Mediterranean blood, to become as involved in *toreo* as I obviously was. I would meet similar incomprehension time and again. Many Spaniards I encountered in the plazas did not want to believe that any foreigner, much less a North American, might understand their special art and speak its language. Spanish nationalism (according to which all pickpockets in Madrid are South Americans) means that simply to be born in Spain endows one with exhaustive knowledge of *toreo.* A distinguished and well-traveled Spanish novelist told me that he could not see how it would be possible to write in English about *toreo.*

On weekends later in my instructional year, Mario, young Mario, aged fourteen, whom his father wanted to succeed him, and one or two other young Mexicans would drive far out in the provinces of Morelia or Guadalajara to *ganaderías,* ranches where the bulls were reared. Ranches near the city were besieged by would-be *novilleros,* lads looking for practice on living animals. In the breeders' *tientas* (testings) we might get a chance to work with the female calves that were being scrutinized for their qualities as breeding stock. In the *tienta,* the animal is released into a small plaza where the efforts of all concerned: the breeder, his mounted vaquero acting as picador, and the *toreros* on foot—are to determine the animals' potentialities, a procedure partly scientific, partly intuitive, and partly mystical. Ideally, the manner of its charge at horse and capes would indicate *casta, codicia,* and whether the animal was *noble,* to name only some of the untranslatable and desirable traits the *ganadero* hoped for.[5]

These engagements needed careful planning, but they often ended in a long drive only to find that the *tienta* would not take place for another month, or that it had been held the previous week. When things went well, those trips were essential to me, no matter how fly-blown the meat and warm the beer pressed on us by the *ganadero,* who often led a chancy existence high on an arid mountain. Practice on a living animal at once revealed how different a fast calf swerving into my body was from an imaginary five-year-old *toro,* and how urgently instinctive reactions interfered with all I had learned from Mario, and how unavoidable were years of experience in observing and discriminating among various strains of the *toro bravo.* The contrast between my mornings and weekends to my late afternoon academic work was complete and compelling. My university hosts were startled; some disapproved of my going so fully native, but were too polite to say so.

June, 1962 approached, and in July I would have to leave Mexico and the bulls to return to life on the eastern seaboard of the United States. My new friends in the world of the bulls, led by Mario, could not believe that I was serious. I had worked hard, and could go on working toward the day when I might even earn big pesos as "El norteamericano" in the plazas along the Texas border. I assured them that I already had a profession, a family to support, and duties to my university and to my students. There was also the little matter of my age, but Mario reminded me that *toreros* had gone on into their fifties and sixties, and hadn't the great Pedro Romero killed bulls in public at the age of eighty? Surely by now I realized that *toreo* was not a sport depending on agility? I indeed knew that, for I had always been enthusiastic but no more than average at tennis, baseball, and other sports.

Finally convinced, Mario and the others set up an "Extraordinario Novillada de Gala" for June 10 in the plaza "La Piedad" in the state of Michoacan, with *novillos* (three-year-old bulls)[6] of Albarrada, a ranch unknown to me and to most people, somewhere up in the mountains.

---

5. *Casta* is a term of high praise. *Codicia* means "greed"; it applies to the *toro* that charges and re-charges with appetite. *Noble* , not a cognate, defines the animal that charges stright to the lure without tossing its horns en route; it is the easiest to *torear.*

6. In a *corrida de toros* the bulls must be four or more years old.

Mario had insisted, with my complicity, that if only for purposes of our book, I must undergo the experience of killing a bull or bulls in public, wearing the *traje de luces* (suit of lights). He also hoped to convince me to renounce university teaching to embark on a belated career in *toreo,* a completely unreal hope.

In the next few weeks I trained with special intensity, dreamt in sweaty nights of tramplings and gorings, and found a tailor who would rent me a tobacco and silver suit for the great day. The suit didn't fit, intended for a shorter man than I was, and it had an ominous repair on the left inner thigh, region of the femoral artery. On the morning of June 9 we set out on the long drive to Michoacan, the Mexicans talking non-stop as always, while I drove, wondering exactly what I had got myself into. What if the rancher was unloading on us a *corrida* of unsalable five-year-old *toros de verdad?* It had been known to happen. We endured several hours on the road, then stopped for some food in a pueblo from which Mario could telephone to check whether the Albarradas in fact were already at La Piedad, calming down in the corrals after their transport by truck.

After a long absence, Mario came back to report that the truck transporting our four bulls had overturned on a mountain road and the *corrida* would have to be suspended. We drove back to Mexico City in silence. We never did learn the fate of the four Albarradas. It was all very Mexican.

It was also very Mexican that the week before I was to leave for good, Mario and the others bought two *novillos* (three-year-olds) for me to *torear* in a small private plaza near Mexico City belonging to a friend. I survived, disgracing neither Mario nor myself, and I am eternally grateful for an extraordinary year among extraordinary people. When it was time to drive away, a dozen of them turned up with farewell presents they could ill afford. Even the hangers-on, some of whom had stolen my best neckties in a party at mid-year, had tears in their eyes, perhaps crocodile tears, that I could really and in truth leave the world of the bulls, the only world that for them had any reality. In due time and after a great deal of further observation in Spanish plazas, a book appeared in the United States and in Britain, written in my English, since Mario knew only Spanish. That in turn led to further critical pieces on *toreo* and to further trips to Spain when the university calendar permitted.

Mexico had been my secondary school and Spain my university in *toreo.* Decades on, some conclusions may be possible, if conclusions are ever possible. No matter where it is practiced, *toreo* remains Spanish in origin and essence, just as Russian opera sung in New York remains Russian. The essence of *toreo* penetrates Spanish behavior in curious and interesting ways. It unfolds on sand in heat or cold, sometimes in wind and rain, and always in bull filth and blood; nevertheless it requires that the matador maintain his posture and his dignity while following an unvarying procedure. That procedure is determined by the nature of the bull and by the history of the matador's craft. He becomes singular, set apart from the run of humanity the moment he steps into the arena. Something of that sense of self, involving honor and *oficio* : an all-important term meaning loyalty to a self-imposed idea of duty—that sense is present in virtually every Spanish man and woman I know. Self-centered to be sure, anarchistic to the marrow, yet courteous and hospitable. "Mi casa es su casa" (my house is your house) they tell you and mean it, but underlying that courtesy is not kindness in our sense, but abstract honor and duty. Such qualities have kept Spain intact in catastrophic times.

My interpretation of Spain, and Mexico, thus mitigated any tendency to idealize *toreo* when I traveled to other countries, but that tendency remained present in myself, for "bullfighting" makes many people nervous, combative, and eager to reform me. They haven't a chance. *Toreo* has given me a view of reality that I have found precious beyond price. In the face of a charging bull, the matador must *aguantar*—endure, suffer—the charge while maintaining his composure. So daily life may charge, horns tossing, and so one must *aguantar* without fleeing in panic. In brief, *toreo* puts things, all things, from trivial to apocalyptic, in proper perspective. For that I am thankful, while remaining unreformed, unrepentant.

8

Searching for Santayana

Long addicted to the various writings of the Spanish philosopher, George Santayana, I found it strange that no one had written the biography that I believed he deserved. His fellow philosophers had turned out the conventional logic-chopping treatises on his philosophy, but they had avoided his work as novelist, essayist, literary and cultural critic, and poet. His autobiographical writing was characteristically urbane and elegant, but partial as autobiography must be. With a mixture of arrogance and bravado, like a man diving into icy water, I determined in 1978 to attempt the missing biography. After two years of preliminary work, I made plans for further research in Spain, Italy, France, and England, countries where Santayana had lived and had had deep attachments. Addicted also to the sea, I arranged to leave from Brooklyn for Piraeus in a Greek container ship, a voyage of thirteen days, then travel by rail and ferry to Italy.

Grigorios proved to be a large ship with a crew of thirty and capacity for nine passengers. After Piraeus she was to touch at Cyprus, Beirut, Thessalonika and Constantine, then return to Brooklyn. On a fine October day I went aboard, installed myself in my cabin, and met the eight other passengers who had joined the ship at Baltimore, elderly retired people taking an economical cruise.

Commanded by her thirty-one-year-old Greek master (who looked sixteen) *Grigorios* cast off mooring lines in the evening and churned into the Atlantic at a smart sixteen knots. Each morning I worked for four or five hours on the first chapter of the book, happy to be at sea again with pleasant, non-intrusive fellow passengers, and a congenial, unsanitary crew of Greeks, Africans, and assorted Mid-Easterners. Four of us passengers had been at sea in professional capacities, including a retired U.S. Naval warrant officer of thirty years' service. I had commanded two small anti-submarine warfare ships during World War II, and I had a master's license in the Merchant Marine, long expired, to be sure.

Common sense, if not previous experience, should have caused us former seamen to protest, even before leaving Brooklyn, that the ship had been loaded to a starboard list. Once under way, I had found the same bucket of cable grease outside my cabin door for five days. The contents of the two lifeboats were strewn about the deck for a week to allow deckhands to paint them; the scuppers were stopped up with waste and usually running with fuel oil. More alarming were the buckets of super-heated bunker oil that appeared outside the door to the stack (funnel) at intervals, slopping over as the ship rolled and rarely swabbed up. Sun, recurrent autumnal gales, squalls, and our status as passengers no doubt blunted our sailorly instincts. For nine days I enjoyed myself, lazing about the deck and reading in the afternoons, in the evenings drinking a whisky with the other passengers, and occasionally with the young Greek master.

On the ninth evening, some 150 miles west of Gibraltar in squalls, heavy winds and a fairly heavy sea, several of us, the master included, had gathered in the small wardroom over our drink. Suddenly, unambiguously, we smelled smoke. The master leapt up, shouting "Be calm, be calm," ran down the companionway, then back again, yelling in unseaman-like manner, "The boat deck. Passengers to the boat deck. Keep calm."

"We are calm," I told him. "You're the one who's excited."

We ignored his order and went instead to our cabins for life jackets. Regretting that there had never been a fire drill or any other sort of drill, I needed several seconds to extract my life jacket, which was jammed between a locker and the overhead. By then smoke from burning plastic was rolling into the cabin through the ventilator and from under the cabin door. Still driving ahead at sixteen knots into the rising gale, *Grigorios* fanned the flames and violated the first rule of fire at sea: stop all engines. Choking, I grabbed a jacket, my wallet, and one of several folders of research notes, which I stuffed down the front of my shirt.

Out on the boat deck, in total darkness sailors were screaming at one another in Greek, Arabic, Swahili, and English. Finally an auxiliary generator was rigged, to illuminate sailors skidding and scrambling on the oily, listing deck, trying to attach fire hoses but uninstructed in use of the necessary wrenches. The former American boatswain did the job for them, but when water pressure finally rose, no water spurted from the unkinked hoses. Engine crew emerged, spewing and spitting, to stand mindlessly about in the wind. The fire had started in the engine room and raged up through the stack to envelop officers' and passengers' quarters and the navigation bridge. The master himself was manning a fire hose, directing salt water, not foam, at the oil fire, as kite-sized hunks of paint flew off the stack. Rescue breathing equipment and respirators were kicking about in the oily mess on deck: a scene from a film directed by Groucho Marx.

Orders came for passengers to abandon ship, but for crew to remain aboard. Because the ship's list had increased, only one lifeboat was launchable. We passengers clambered into the boat, while the coxswain tossed in whichever essentials came to hand. Fire hoses shot water at the white-hot stack, at the trembling sailors, and at us in the lifeboat, swinging on the davits but impossible to launch while the ship careened along at speed. After hours, or minutes, time was the time of dreams, the ship slowed, than hove to, permitting our descent into a boiling sea. The davit rocker arms, which should have remained attached to the davits, came away with us, gashing a woman's arm. A shackle attaching the cable fall to the lifeboat was frozen with rust, causing the boat to swing about alarmingly; I tackled the cable fall to prevent it from braining a woman seated near it. Astern of the ship at last, but still attached to her by a hawser, we saw the portholes of our cabins blow out in arcs into the sea, like white-hot footballs. So much for two year's research notes and forty pages of typescript, to say nothing of irreplaceable books, typewriter, my Leica camera, and luggage full of clothing.

Four crewmen took it on themselves to abandon ship, launching an inflatable raft. Two men swung from the ship's stern all night on a paint pontoon, while two others clung to rope ladders, too frightened or too weak to move. The obedient who remained aboard were able to confine the fire to the amidships area by playing water on the containers topside and on the cargo-hold hatch covers. For the next twenty hours we remained attached to the ship by hawser, careening in the seas in motion that made the landsmen among us seasick. The men took turns with an oar to fend off the ship's counter, under which we were drawn as the seas heaved the stern high over our heads.

Toward dawn the Kenyan coxswain announced, apropos of nothing, "Trouble in airplane, *every* body die. Trouble in ship, *no* body die." This had been contradicted by one of the oilers, who said that two men had not left the engine room. His statement was never confirmed or denied by the shipping line. Dawn showed us great billows of black smoke rising from *Grigorios;* dawn also showed us that we had navigational charts only for Arctic waters, a dubious compass, one small container of fresh water, and a lump of chocolate. There were flares and a flare gun, but no spare fuel for the motor. The four women shared two sodden blankets. The unspoken thought in all our minds was that if the ship went down, we might be in unvarnished, bleak trouble.

We shot off our six flares at half-hourly intervals, believing, as the Greek master had assured me, that we were in the shipping lanes: we were not, as it turned out. At long length *Samos,* a Greek grain ship underway from the Black Sea to New Orleans appeared on the horizon, and as she approached, my previous anxiety about survival turned slowly into anger at the chaos we had seen aboard *Grigorios.* After we had literally been picked out of the lifeboat by the crew of *Samos,* we learned that our ship's distress signal had given a position wrong by forty miles. *Samos* had smelled smoke from twenty miles off and may have seen the last of our flares on the horizon. Our boat could not be hauled up conventionally from the sea on davits because of the ship's rolling in the high seas, compounded by her being in ballast and riding high over the water. Crewmen from *Grigorios* who had moved from their raft to the lifeboat trampled the old people to scramble up a cargo net. Eight passengers had to be hoisted up the side on lines, like bales of cotton; in sinful pride I disdained a line and went up the jabob's ladder on my own, but I hoped that Santayana might have been proud of his biographer.

Samos passed the next forty-eight hours in piratically circling the still smoking *Grigorios,* her master believing he could claim her as derelict, therefore his booty: technically she was not derelict, for the master and a few men remained aboard, continually wetting down cargo. The owners of the two ships quarreled in Piraeus, while gales blew both ships in the direction of Casablanca. Eventually a Dutch tug took the smoking ship in tow and headed north. *Samos* had no quarters for passengers. The women were given berths in the small sick-bay, and their husbands, one of whom looked very ill, dossed down on deck, as did I, until an engineer offered me his bunk when he was on watch. It was airless and reeked of oil, and I regretted his hospitality but could not refuse it for fear of offending him.

Two full days after we had been picked up, the master appeared, welcomed us aboard, and said that in eight days or so we would be back on native soil, in New Orleans. The former warrant officer and I protested: old and apparently sick people might not survive that journey, and in any case he well knew that he was obliged, in international waters, to put us off at the nearest port having appropriate accommodations. He was much put out at meeting a couple of sea-lawyers, but finally he agreed. Four days after our rescue, at 3 A.M. in a warm rain, we were deposited on a lighter off Funchal, Madeira, where we were greeted by the honorary British consul, dressed in his school blazer and tie. The honorary consul's first question was, "Now tell me, please, would you good people prefer hard or medium tooth-brushes?" I thought for a moment that I was a character in a novel by Graham Greene. We soon convinced the man that what we needed first was lodging and clothes, and to his credit he at once arranged for a dry goods store to open up at 4 a.m. and made reservations in hotels. I found that I was the only one among us to have wallet and passport; I was able to leave Madeira four days later for Lisbon and New York. My fellow passengers waited two and more weeks for passports and money.

Before we parted, we agreed that since I was the only passenger living in the east, I should find an admiralty lawyer and discuss a group action against the shipping line for negligence. I wanted to know what had become of *Grigorios,* having been assured that she was being towed to Gibraltar for repairs. She was not at Gibraltar, I learned by telephoning a friend in Spain whose relative worked there. Another friend in Athens sent me a brief newspaper clipping describing the heroism of the young Greek master and his crew in saving the ship and her cargo from a fearsome fire at sea. The item was not picked up by the wire services nor was any mention of our tribulations ever reported in the world press. That seemed unusual. When fire broke out aboard the Italian cruise ship, *Achille Lauro,* all but two of her 1,000 passengers were rescued before the ship foundered, an event widely and melodramatically reported in all media. Reasons for the disparity in treatment of the two disasters were long in coming to light, and only opaque light at that.

After four years of Jarndyce vs. Jarndyce arguments in the admiralty lawyers' offices, the shipping line settled, parsimoniously, out of court. During that action, it became clear, *Grigorios* had loaded munitions for Beirut at Baltimore, stenciling the wooden cases "rags"; and at last I could account for the Greek master's unmanly excitement when we smelled smoke. A letter to the State Department requesting a copy of *Grigorios'* manifest, significantly, went unanswered. At least *Achille Lauro* went to the bottom with a clean manifest, it seems.

Two morals emerge: beware of Greeks running ships; and scholars in your ivory tower, choose your subject with caution, for you never know when or what sort of fire may break out.

9

Brutality in Biography

Research and writing a biography of Santayana, in conjunction with teaching, occupied eight years, in which time I thought a great deal about the nature of biography: what it so often is, what it ideally ought to be, and the particular difficulties that genre posed for anyone writing the life of a person in the arts. That which biographers and the reading public found palatable had obviously changed since Plutarch led the way, but changes in the years after 1960 seemed to have altered a central aesthetic, reflecting a coarsened taste in what was to be offered as correctness in interpretation of an outstanding individual.

Publishers' practices are such that biographies come and biographies go to the remainder tables, some among them bringing handsome rewards to their authors, others bringing little but years of work, and to publishers financial loss. The money-makers are usually salted with sexual minutiae in the lives of the rich, the famous, or the notorious infamous. Sly smuttiness about the prominent is hardly new, but titillation in the name of candor is new. Of late, many professional, scholarly biographers have rejected the discretion, tact, and circumlocutions of the past in preference for the surgical, sexual details that once lay unmentioned or only obliquely paraphrased from the subject's most private records. The disappearance of the once clear line between the biographer who aspired to permanence and the biographer who aspired to rewarding impermanence relates to that period when suddenly the noun f-u-c-k as verb, participle and gerund sent a *frisson* into "the upper depths" of society.[1] Why that small revolution, small but significant, occurred is for the sociologists and moral philosophers to determine, but some of its results may be worth recording here.

In the thirty years from 1970 to the end of the century, biographies of W.H. Auden, Oscar Wilde, Ernest Hemingway, Robert Lowell, Federico García Lorca, William Faulkner, Somerset Maugham, Graham Greene, Eric Gill, Thomas Mann, to list only a few, are remarkable mainly for documented material or surmise about the aberrations of their subjects, material which, in more decorous times, would have been considered marginal at best. In Humphrey Carpenter's *W.H. Auden,* the poet is not the master of form and diction we might prefer to recall, but a voracious, cruising homosexual whose tastes and practices are listed at such length and lubricity that the undoubted stature of Auden the artist sinks from view. So good a scholar and writer as Richard Ellmann found it necessary to trace Wilde's seductions of man and boy in punctilious and repellent detail, even though Wilde's ways have been known for decades. Maugham, the most private of men in life, has been mercilessly violated after his death in the name of openness about homosexual liaisons.

As for American writers, Hemingway has been proposed not as a writer whose best work influenced American prose style profoundly, but as a would-be trans-sexual with a fixation on hair. As more and more is written about Faulkner, so less and less attention goes to his work in favor of his wanderings outside marriage and his consumption of whisky. Ian Hamilton's *Robert Lowell* devotes an inordinate amount of space to Lowell's illness and to his various foibles. T.S. Eliot, still an American writer in my book, has been spared trial by documented biography because his widow has not released his private papers, but dark hints indicate that the days of such reticence are numbered.

On the continent, we have Thomas Mann and García Lorca to consider. Ronald Hayman's *Thomas Mann* runs to 672 pages, or by rough count, 266,000 words. Such inordinate length is not the result of Hayman's exhaustive literary enquiry into Mann's art, but extensive reliance on Hayman's translations and paraphrases of Mann's private diaries, often written in code to conceal his sexual life, by turns or simultaneously heterosexual and homosexual. The entire reason for the biography would appear to rest on the availability in the mid-1990s in Germany of Mann's diaries, together with collections of letters formerly withheld. Hayman pretends to objectivity, but the imbalance between prurience and commonly known facts about Mann is so great that his genuine stature as an artist is diminished, if not shattered. One comes away from Hayman's book with an image of

Thomas Mann as a cross between sublime idiot and utter swine, hardly the result that the industrious Hayman intended, it would seem.

In his huge *Federico Garcîa Lorca,* already the subject of more biographical and critical studies than any other Spanish writer, Ian Gibson duplicates the dubious triumph of Ronald Hayman. Presuming to provide an exhaustive study of the poet's life and work, he gives as much space to guess-work about Garcîa Lorca's male lovers, their names and positions in society, including details about Lorca's physical position in his supposed acts of sodomy, as to Lorca's writings. Since the Spain of Lorca's lifetime (1898–1936) was a place of decorum and hypocrisy, Gibson was forced to derive his evidence from words or lines of verse, and from ingenious readings of scraps of correspondence. Perhaps one-half of the biography is written in the conditional, a characteristic of the scurrilous genre.

In 1998 poor Lorca, who was after all a major and memorable poet, was again subjected to tedious scrutiny in Miss Leslie Stainton's *Lorca: A Dream of Life* Miss Stainton not only repeats Ian Gibson's prurience, but she also adds enormously to his sexual detail, the result of her having access to papers previously unavailable. The result is 568 pages of repetitious and unorganized scrutiny, with only occasional attention to what matters: Lorca's poetry. The book is saved from being a compilation of facts (not in the conditional for once) by the writer's good grasp of the historical background, particularly her adeptness in addressing the complexities of the Civil War.

The case of Eric Gill, typographer, sculptor of erotic kitsch, author of social polemic and self-proclaimed aspirant to sainthood may offer special insight into the scholarly/scurrilous genre. Two biographies had already been published, but Fiona MacCarthy added a third in 1989, *Eric Gill.* At his death in 1940, Gill had left notebooks recording his extensive sexual encounters, encompassing incest and animalism. His earlier biographers knew about the notebooks, which were made fully available to Robert Speaight, for his biography of 1966. Both earlier biographers alluded to Gill's peculiar sexual adventures without quoting the salacious notebooks. In a full exhibition of the new sensibility, Fiona MacCarthy published an article about her work, "Why It Must Now Be Warts and All," writing that discretion in sexual matters equals "wilful suppression," and adding, "I can still capture that strange prickling of the spine as I read through Gill's diaries and sexual confessions in Southern California in 1986." (The syntax here reflects Fiona MacCarthy's fevered state.) The task, then, is to discover why it was that Speaight's spine did not prickle, as Fiona MacCarthy's so memorably did? Even to ask the question and to have cast doubt on the biographical judgment of such as Carpenter, Ellmann, and the rest is to risk sounding like a reformed smoker who cannot bear even matches; or at best a Malvolio-like stuffed shirt.

Without holding myself up as a model biographer, I offer the kinds of difficulty posed for the biographer in the career of a most complex man, George Santayana. In his character and work, contradictory qualities commingled in ways difficult for the biographer to map. Because of his birth and early upbringing in Spain, he did not learn English until age nine in a Boston kindergarten, yet he wrote prose in English that must rank with the finest for lucidity, range, and clarity. Student, instructor, then professor of philosophy at Harvard, he retired at age forty-nine, for temperamental and intellectual dislike of universities and most of his colleagues. His many books set forth an individual philosophy, but he refused to engage in philosophical argument, thus committing virtual professional suicide. He was a metaphysical naturalist, or a naturalistic metaphysician. Aristocratic in demeanor and conservative in politics, he wrote a best-selling novel and read the writings of Stalin in Italian with interest and (puzzling) pleasure.

Santayana also wrote superb essays and letters, indifferent verse drama, a few fine sonnets, a study called *The Idea of Christ in the Gospels,* and a vast book of political and historical analysis, *Dominations and Powers.* He sought out Bostonian society when young, belonging to some eleven undergraduate organizations at Harvard. A student of William James and Josiah Royce, he met Henry James and knew well many of the eminent of his time in America, England, and on the continent. He never dropped names, unlike his friend Bertrand Russell (who not only dropped but bounced them), and never elbowed his way: he forbade acquaintances to put his name forward for a Nobel Prize. In his thirties he abruptly withdrew from society, and left America altogether on his retirement. He considered himself an American writer but retained Spanish citizenship throughout his long life: 1863–1952. Born Catholic, his naturalism led him to atheism early on (as I have noted in chapter 2). He was an anti-Semite, an Anglophile, a learned, congenially aloof man, generous, witty, and in spite of his blind spots, wonderfully intelligent.

Such qualities presented the biographer with difficulties of interpretation and organization, which with luck and time could be overcome. Disturbing difficulty arose, as it so commonly does, in matters political and sexual. After Santayana's death, his literary executor, Daniel Cory, published a volume of letters and various biographical memoirs from which he deleted any unpleasant references to the Jews, and with one exception, anything that might be construed as referring to sex. As for politics, I thought it essential to establish that Santayana had indeed been an anti-Semite, that his customary decency and humanity failed him when he approved of Céline's appalling rant against the Jews, or when he wrote to his nephew that the Jews "are just sheenies." He believed that communists in the United States were all Jews, as was the New York literary establishment. So peculiar and out of character were these and many more examples that I was tempted, fleetingly, to suppress them as mere aberration. Tempering my previous admiration for Santayana, I wrote a full account of that unpleasant chapter in the man's life. Not to have done so would have been to play false with the documented evidence, to say nothing of my own peace of mind.

The sexual matter was of an entirely different nature. Although I was convinced that Santayana was homosexual by inclination and was probably celibate, the evidence is only inferential, in his novel, in letters, in some of his verse, and in a few marginalia. His warmest friendships were with men, preferably young and handsome men. He liked women and corresponded all his life with several Boston matrons whom he had known as a young man, but clearly he did not love women and was amusingly evasive whenever the question of marriage arose. He was candid about sex in his letters, on the few occasions the subject arose. Once only he displayed what must be taken as duplicity about the nature and meaning of homosexuality: according to Daniel Cory, Santayana said to him in 1929 about A.E. Housman's poetry, "'I suppose Housman was really what people nowadays call ""homosexual,"' and he went on to say as if he were speaking to himself: "'I think I must have been that way in my Harvard days—although I was unconscious of it at the time.'"

Accordingly, it would have been possible to paste together in the conditional mode, through intuition and inference from various writ-

---

1. See Saul Bellow's play of that title.

ings, a case for Santayana as active homosexual.[2] I found many reasons against that procedure. The first was a residual historical memory that from Plutarch to Boswell and Carlyle, biographies were written and read mainly as *exempla,* moral homilies for how human life should or should not be lived. By the mid-nineteenth century, biography in Britain and America had become modified to Kantian idealism as enunciated by Fichte and Schelling, to emerge as Carlyle's lectures of 1837–1840, "On Heroes, Hero-Worship, and the Heroic in History." In America, Ralph Waldo Emerson, under Carlyle's influence as well as the Germans', produced *Representative Men* in 1850, after long meditation on heroism and human greatness. Scientific determinism from Darwin to Freud of course finished off efforts to interpret human activity as inspired by romantic heroism. People who had never heard of Darwin or Freud reached their own conclusions about inspired heroic leaders when they considered the results achieved by the politicians and generals of World War I, by the fascist politicians of Europe and Japan between the wars, or the allied leaders of World War II, whose mistakes appeared to outnumber their triumphs. For us Americans, Vietnam famously led to unparalleled cynicism among young and old concerning the very possibility of idealism among politicians and the professional military. Biography as *exemplum* was a practice that history had eliminated, even while there remained as many, or as few, admirable people as there ever had been. Public attitudes and political conditions rather than character had changed.

The anti-heroic, anti-hagiographical mode in biography, long overdue, became dominant in English with Lytton Strachey's *Eminent Victorians* (1918), and his life of Queen Victoria (1921). Although pseudo-elegant, snide, and amateur to many readers, Strachey's writings nevertheless marked his generation heavily. Despite their inconoclasm, biographers of Strachey's persuasion still maintained decorum in diction, and the pretence of fairness and objectivity. From the 1930s until well after World War II, the predominance of the New Criticism, particularly in the United States, meant neglect of biographical interpretation and consequent neglect of biography itself. By 1960, the New Criticism had been long forgotten; the confessional mode in verse and autobiography spilled over into biographies, which prolifer-

---

2. That had been done: Robert K. Martin, *Tradition in American Poetry* (Austin: University of Texas Press, 1979), pp. 108–114.

ated, and at the same time, the two approaches, the scholarly and the scurrilous, merged, like river water merging with the salt sea.

While thinking about Santayana, I recalled the words of Claude-Edmonde Magny a generation ago in her article, "Finalement." The French critic asks whether the great dead "belong" to us, whether we are granted any right as biographers and readers to sort through Goethe's laundry lists or to tally Flaubert's visits to the bordellos. Implicit is the notion that if we violate human privacy, even the privacy of the dead, we reduce and cheapen ourselves. What matters, what leads the biographer to write, is the achievement, not the foibles of the subject. One objection to Claude-Edmonde Magny's high-minded view is that it is at once human and scholarly to want to know all, warts and weaknesses, about a biographer's subject. Any attempt at whitewash must fail, for whitewash soon flakes away in any case. At issue is the ritualistic, automatic descriptions of sexual experience, amounting to caricature, at the expense of balance and fullness in the completed portrait.

A corollary of that view is to consider biography as a form of history. Since genuine history requires the perspective of time (without which it is no more than compilation of data), so genuine biography also requires time, that sorting-out process that data mysteriously undergo with the passage of decades. Such a view rules out the hot-off-the-press "biography" of a presidential candidate, or of the latest phenomenon in sport or finance. It also rules out the recently dead. The historian and the biographer need filtering time[3] in order to see in depth, to compare, to contrast, and to try to record in three dimensions rather than one.

Another reason for not dwelling on Santayana's sexual preferences is a conviction that we are too ready to believe that everything in human character can and must be explained, either by chemistry, biology, psychoanalysis, water-cures, aroma therapy, Alcoholics Anonymous, plastic inserts, or liver-packs. Such a propensity defies all genuine art and much of human experience, in which mystery, insoluble and perhaps annoying, simply does exist. As someone remarked, the biographer knows more about his subject than the subject in life could know about himself. That knowledge may tempt the biographer to the deadly sin of pride, which causes him to fit his evidence into expli-

---

3. Groucho Marx had a point with his remark, "Time wounds all heels."

cable categories, and to ignore his intuition, if he is honest, that he cannot know all about anybody. Human personality finally remains walled about by the unknowable, and a good thing it is.

In contrast to Carpenter's treatment of Auden or Fiona MacCarthy's of Eric Gill are other biographies of the same period of people who led lurid lives, but whose achievements predominate in our minds over their unusual private tastes. George D. Painter's two-volume *Marcel Proust* (1959–1965) is candid about Proust's adventures, but Painter is neither prurient nor prissy in his treatment; his book remains an achievement. The same applies to Leslie A. Marchand's *Byron: A Portrait* (1971). Even more than Proust's, Byron's roamings can obscure his poetry, since readers now need devotion and study to appreciate Byron's idiom and technique. It is easier to recall his travelling zoo, his suspected incest, his mistresses and all those boys, than to wrestle with Byron's literary achievement. Marchand suppresses nothing, neither does he wallow. He is literary, lively, scholarly, and never pompous.

It is hardly necessary to argue that public censorship is a mistake, as is the self-censorship that would suppress any facts that aid the understanding of character, accomplishment, or lack of accomplishment. The issue is not suppression, as Fiona MacCarthy asserts, but one of balance and selection. All biographers select, and by definition, reject material. If biography is a branch of history, as I believe it must be, it also approaches art in that the portrait presented to the reader, if it is to endure, must be based in fastidious research, but finally it can only be imaginary: the result of the intellect, industry, intuition, and imagination of the biographer. Unlike prose fiction, biography is subject to limits, the limits of reality itself. And it is deeply subject to the sensibility of the biographer.

Looking back, one may see with some degree of historical rather than anecdotal clarity that between 1965 and 1975, public attitudes toward sexual matters shifted significantly. That shift was inescapably obvious in the United States, although it also occurred in Britain and in Western Europe with varying degrees of acceleration. Apparently infallible techniques of contraception gave the young the illusion of choice, of freedom from past constraints. Women of all ages believed themselves to have been liberated as never before from ancient tyrannies: to men, to marriage, to the pretence of universal heterosexuality. Homosexuality came to be considered as healthy and was made legal;

only the appearance of AIDS had a negative effect on those seemingly irreversible changes.

It appears beyond challenge that alterations in our very thought-processes, resulting from "liberation," if that is the word, have had extraordinary effects on our literature and our daily, demotic language. What was once a subterranean argot reserved to foul moments of stress, to men in combat, or to dirty jokes has become banality at the dinner table, the theater, on television, in verse, and in prose. Imaginative cussing, an art form now unfamiliar, is a thing of the past. Such verbal "liberation" suggests a thickening of our public and private rind, the virtual elimination of our public sensibility. So strident a voice as Susan Sontag's assured us that sensibility had indeed changed, and that now it had become "defiantly pluralistic." In the history of philosophy, "pluralistic" has usually been a circumlocution for "anything goes," which in turn was crudely reduced to "let it all hang out." Miss Sontag's words were thus a benediction to insensibility. The resulting brutalization of public diction may be related to the brutalization of intellectual diction, under the influence of Foucault, Derrida, and the entire French-inspired, anti-logical and anti-intellectual school of American fish swimming in those French waters.

Logically, then, changes in biography registered a deep intellectual brutality at work. Changes in diction are a ready measure of the new intellectual brutality, I suspect. Diction in prose is no less a measure of mind and sensibility than it is in poetry. Diction is to prose as color is to painting, but circumlocution is to obscenity as clothes to nakedness. In his memoirs, Donald Davie wrote that he found the common currency of obscenities "an affront." They are an affront, I think, because they are reductive, anti-élitist, and no more than intellectual slumming on the page of the serious biographer. A character in Iris Murdoch's novel, *The Message to the Planet* remarks, "honest, truth-bearing ordinary language, *that's* what we've got to save." The question of how much is enough? will not down. How many more reductive, off-balance studies do we need of the Bloomsbury group, or of William Faulkner, or of García Lorca? No one can or should prescribe how to write biography, nor can any biography pretend to what publishers like to tout as definitive. But without insisting on a return to the asterisk, we can cry out when affronted.

10

Retiring Abroad

In university teaching and in related professions, many pay homage to the notion that wisdom increases with age, not least their own. Lacking illusions about my own wisdom, I retired from teaching eighteen months before I had to, partly because I found it increasingly hard to break down the barriers of difference between my students and me. Distaste for male scruffiness set off by earrings was hard to conceal, and the sight of young women in running suits and punk hairdos made it wearying to lecture or to induce discussion of my subject. My diction puzzled the undergraduates, and theirs aroused my incredulity. Although it sounds pious, I thought it unfair to occupy a senior position when the profession was glutted with good young people who could not find a job. If it hadn't been for children of my own to see through university, I would have retired even earlier. Practicality apart, the conscious decision to retire early means not being turned out for bureaucratic reason; the initiative is on the self: a healthier place for it, surely.

Having seen colleagues retire, only to remain in houses they had inhabited for years, among surviving friends of decades, where they tried to carry on their habitual activities in their habitual surroundings only to go out with a despairing sigh, I came to think that my retirement should also include removal to new surroundings. To remain might involve that slow fading, no matter what one's efforts to maintain habits and connections subtly in flux. M agreed that to remove our persons and possessions was a calculated risk, but one offering either interesting gains or disaster. Either attracted us more than the fading aridity implicit in staying on. Passivity is expected in the aging, but passivity may encourage arthritic stiffness in body and mind.

The reactions of friends to one's decisions matter; thus I was concerned that some appeared upset that I, an American, Minnesota born, should choose to live and probably die abroad, far from the customary skies. No one used the word, but some implied that I was being unpatriotic. It was the literal *trahison* of a single *clerc,* me. Our intention was appropriate for M, who would be returning to her English roots after thirty years in foreign parts, and a few friends concluded darkly that I was being shanghaied by my wife. My roots were shallow, even by American standards, but my affection for Britain and Western Europe was deep. I was not being shanghaied.

We encountered incomprehension at the idea of retirement to Yorkshire. London or the familiar south of England would have made sense to most of our friends, for in spirit they agreed with Sydney Smith: "All lives out of London are mistakes." Weren't we choosing a backwater? Possibly, I answered, but I had never found life in the front water as exhilarating as the magazine *Vanity Fair* would have us believe. "Yorkshire?" a woman asked, "Won't you be cold? Where is it?" If Yorkshire exists at all in most Americans' minds, it is the Yorkshire of the West Riding, the *Wuthering Heights* country of Heathcliff, Cathy's ghost, and howling winds.

The appearance and recent disappearance of the word "Riding" may be confusing. Contemporary Yorkshire has a population equal to Scotland's and a sense of itself as a geographical and cultural entity less noisy but equal in intensity to that of the Scots. For geographical and administrative reasons dating from the ninth century, the region was divided into thirds, North, East and West, "Riding" meaning a third part and derived from Old Norse and late Old English. With the efforts of successive Labour and Conservative governments to reform local government, new administrative units appeared having little geographical logic, and with them, a nomenclature devised to eliminate the ancient (and beautiful) terminology.[1] The struggle to reform the reforms goes on; a movement is in progress as I write (1999) to achieve autonomy for Yorkshire and to reclaim the Ridings.

The part of the North Riding we chose to settle in begins just north

---

1. The former Ridings at the time of writing are North Yorkshire, West Yorkshire, and Humberside. In 1997, succeeded in causing their Riding to be renamed East Yorkshire.

of the city of York, less than two hours by train from London and just over two hours to Edinburgh. After an intense search, we found part of a huge Georgian house of circa 1750, with a garden and woodland, lying in rolling farmland, and within walking distance of Scackleton (ten houses, a church, a mail box) and Hovingham, population 320. York is eighteen miles off, and the moors, snow-covered in winter and heather-purple in late summer, lie within a fifteen minute drive, readily visible on good days. We have owls in the garden by night and indignant pheasants by day, as well as many races of songbirds, including one that sounds like the nerve-flaying ringing of an English telephone. Much of the surrounding land has been owned by the same family since Elizabethan days and farmed by successive generations of the same tenant farming families. They raise potatoes, grain, and hay for sheep and cattle, and for the horses of the gentry who hunt, or for the racehorses that are bred nearby. The North Riding, like all Yorkshire, has been inhabited for as long as mankind has existed in Northern Europe: tumuli rise everywhere in the countryside. Much suffering has been endured in the Yorkshire landscape; it has been fought over and died for.

Hovingham and Scackleton are listed in the Domesday Book. Five miles off is Vanbrugh's Castle Howard, and not much farther lie the Cistercian abbeys of Rievaulx, Byland, and Fountains, destroyed in the Reformation but still haunting and impressive in their ruins. Laurence Sterne wrote *Tristram Shandy* in his vicarage at Coxwold, a dozen miles away. ("Shandy" in Yorkshire dialect means "crazy.") Richard Sterne, his great-grandfather, died at eighty-seven, still in office as Archbishop of York, and a reminder that in the past people did not retire.

The Romans made York into a major military headquarters. York Minster, which dominates the city and the surrounding Vale of York, is one of the finest cathedrals in Europe. A church stood on the site from the early seventh century to 1154, when the cathedral proper was begun. Astonished by the medieval city walls, one of our American visitors asked, "Is York for real?"

Like the surrounding hamlets, settlements, and villages, the city is indeed real, not reconstructed, like Williamsburg, to duplicate the past, but evidence that the past can survive and flourish despite invasions and wars, foreign and civil. Guy Fawkes and W.H. Auden were born in York; Constantine the Great was proclaimed Caesar there in 306.

Seven miles west of the city lies Marston Moor, site in 1644 of a decisive victory of the Parliamentary forces over the Royalists in the Civil War. Sir Thomas (later Lord) Fairfax, one of the victorious commanders at the battle, was to become "my Lord General," commander-in-chief of all Commonwealth armies. It was on his estate at Nun Appleton, close by York, that Andrew Marvell wrote his most perfect poems while tutor to Mary Fairfax, the Lord General's daughter. The Yorkshire Ridings are the country of William Etty, Henry Moore, and Herbert Read. Turner painted there, and John Sell Cotman carved his nickname on a tree at Brandsby. In *Parade's End,* Ford Madox Ford's finely imagined character, Tietjens, is a Yorkshireman.

For an American visitor, the indubitable reality of York and its environs may be put in question by the impression that in both urban and rural North and East Ridings one has returned to what late nineteenth-century or early twentieth-century small-town America must have been. That impression persists despite modern farm machinery, cars, mostly new, on every road, and the proliferation of all the devices of instant communication. The causes for that impression are many, but most immediate are the dominance of landscape, of solid and beautiful buildings, and of a tempo and organization of life that contradict the logic of the mobile telephone, e-mail, and twenty-four hour television news. Where life whizzes by in the new world, it loafs along in the old. No matter how preoccupied, people pause to acknowledge one another, if only with the smallest of small talk. There is less knowingness than in the United States, less surface glitter. Children tend to remain children until adulthood (although that is changing rapidly). No one kicks the dog, and the birds are tame. No matter its reputation, the weather is more benign than not. In summer the air is that of a New England spring; in winter, the sun does not really rise, but slides along the horizon before slipping away.

The people of the North Riding are remarkably homogeneous. They tend to have long waists, short stout legs, and blue eyes in ruddy faces. They have heard of cholesterol but ignore it. They drink quantities of the good local beer, and while they are often tubby, they are rarely obese. Their posture is erect. They walk fast and far and produce good athletes. The most alarming danger in York is that of being rammed by a double pram pushed at speed through the narrow, crowded medieval streets. There are no graffiti, but a welcome absence of the mindless obscenities of American city streets.

Not that Yorkshiremen are puritanical. A menu states that the management has "no objection to discreet breast-feeding in the restaurant." It adds, genteelly, "However, please be understanding if other customers do object." A walk in the main thoroughfare of York on a warm summer evening produced the sight of a group of people drinking outside a pub. Two young women, laughing the hooting workingwoman's laugh, took turns baring the other's bottom and spanking it smartly. Frankness about sexual matters in the English press makes the American press seem quaint, an attitude that carries over to television, wholesale: gaminess rules.

One joy of retirement to our part of Yorkshire is that we may choose as much or as little of city life, or of television, as we wish. Often we look to the moors just to the north, high peat lands, uncultivated and inhabited by horned sheep, grouse, and skylarks. The absence of trees, fences, or power lines opens expanses of sky and cloud, producing the illusion that one is at sea. In some of the steep folds of the moor one comes upon settlements, apparently timeless, always watered by a stream and marked by a medieval church, more or less restored, a shop doubling as a post office, a pub, and a few well-kept stone cottages. On Bransdale moor lies Cockayne Rigg (ridge), hardly the abode of luxury and idleness of medieval legend, but a place carved by wind and rain, bleak but beautiful. The beauty of the moors does not leap out. It is an acquired taste, demanding waterproof boots and patient observation in all weathers.

Our mid-eighteenth-century stone house needed work. The previous owner, an alcoholic man of business who had wrapped his Jaguar around a tree and broken his neck, was not given to maintenance. The joiner (carpenter), the plasterer, the painter, the plumber, the electrician, and the furnace man introduced me to a language and a way of life that to the tourist or occasional brief tenant remains concealed. To the craftsmen I was an old foreigner with a lot of books. They showed me respect, an open, at first reserved, friendliness, and politeness without a vestige of truckling. The older men were almost courtly, in contrast to many workmen in the United States who call you by your first name and are breezily superior to your ignorance of their craft. I learned the Yorkshireman's great pride in his workmanship, and his pleasure in my pleasure at good results.

To save money and for exercise I did a fair amount of work myself. I found that my American screwdrivers were useless, for British screws have narrower slots than ours. I came to admire the design of British wheelbarrows, which have a lower center of gravity, hence are more stable and less fatiguing than ours. In the course of putting down new flooring in a bathroom, I managed to drive four nails through copper water pipes. While M tried to stem the spurting hot water, I looked in vain for the shut-off valve and called the plumber. He came at once, although it was a Saturday evening. I expressed my self-contempt and apologized for interrupting his tea (dinner), but he reassured me: "I've done it in me own house to pipes I put in meself." When his bill arrived, he had added no surcharge for the after-hours emergency work.

American east coast abrasiveness is rare to nonexistent in Yorkshire. Occasional abruptness is usually followed by a smile and an explanation. I discovered that if I wore a tie when buying supplies in the Saturday market at Malton, I was elevated to the peerage: "Bananas, milord?" the woman in the fruit stall would ask. Low comedy, but how much nicer than low rudeness. I have been instructed by a bus driver resembling a heavyweight boxer to "Move back in the saloon please luv." The joiner called his step-ladder his "mount," and when I offered to hang up his jacket, he threw it on the floor, saying "We call that 'Charley Moorman's peg.'" He had no idea who Charley Moorman was. A blowsy-looking but very nice blond cashier in a grocery warned me not to confuse a five-pence piece for a one-pound coin. "If you do, they'll take you for a tá ta." Her tá ta was Bertie Wooster's ta tá, for goodbye. A loose translation would be, "They'll take you for a ride." In small shops clerks still know mental arithmetic, but in supermarkets, the calculator has taken over.

The homogeneity of the North and East Ridings reflects the predominance of agriculture, as opposed to the West Riding, where the industrial revolution began and persists, drawing immigrants from the Caribbean, Africa, and Asia. The factories of Leeds and Bradford that attract the immigrant contrast with the pronounced feudal atmosphere of the North and East Ridings, where the middle class arrived late in time and few in number, and where the industrial West Riding is held in unspoken but definite contempt. But like the Welsh and the Scots, Yorkshiremen in all Ridings have retained their ways and expressions. Yorkshire is their *patria,* the place for which they have fought in astonishing numbers. When the volunteer armies were formed at the beginning of the First World War, entire miners' clubs, entire populations of the young in village after village enlisted and went to be slaughtered. In a single regiment, the King's Own Yorkshire Light Infantry, 9,447 were killed in that war. The history of the regiment was essentially repeated in World War II. Yorkshiremen resist immigration to the south, where the money is. A York man back from London said it was a place "where they call you 'sir' and rip you off." Bleak villages adjacent to abandoned coal mines are populated by people on the dole, unwilling to leave ancestral turf, the men often too old for the government's retraining schemes.

I do not intend to praise England at the expense of my own country, but comparison is inevitable, often odious, and sly when only implied. Many of our daily exchanges are comparisons in varying degrees of invidiousness, depending upon the sweetness of our natures and the measure of good or evil fortune allotted to us. And when does odious comparison cross over to genuine discrimination, that mark of true education? It remains pointless to compare old York to New York, a pseudo-sociological folly. It is often the case that the visitor misreads the signals in a foreign land. At hand is an account of four years in Washington, D.C. by a reporter for the London Sunday newspaper, the *Observer.* Robert Chesshyre in *Return of a Native Reporter* informs us that his friends did not lock their doors when they went out (in *Washington?),* and that the majority of high school graduates had not been daunted by school but stimulated. He remarks that the very garages he saw in Washington are larger than an English drawing room.

It is pleasant to read praise of our country, but praise based on misunderstanding is another matter. Chesshyre praises our democracy and lack of snobbery. To my mind, we are as snobbish as the British, but our kind runs on rails of a different gauge. American snobbery is subtler than the British variety and more insidious as a result. British snobbery, by which most people mean class distinction, is traditional, it carries well-known and unmistakable markings. Ours combines regard for blood and family with much greater regard for money and possessions, with gradations according to education and accent that few foreigners can or do fathom. It is easier to move around in our society than in Britain, but that ease pertains more to our numbers and geography than to our practice of democracy. In the genuine regard of one human being for another that exists in the North Riding, I would give odds that Britain may be more genuinely democratic than we Americans are.

Chesshyre's account of returning to Britain in 1986 only duplicates reports of well-informed analysts by the dozen who have substantiated and expanded upon his words: he found unmitigated despair among the young, poverty and resignation among working-class adults, intolerance, pettiness, snobbery and narrowness of vision. Others have added racial hatred, insularity, and the arrogance of a once-great empire attempting to carry more weight in world affairs than is justified or sensible. I see prosperity and confidence, apart from the mining villages, and an island of sociological peace here in the North. The middle-aged and the old whom I know have accepted Britain's post-imperial status, while the young in general lack the historical knowledge to care.

To be sure, Britain is beset with troubles, but the informing difference between our two countries is that British troubles are subject to rational analysis and often get it. American troubles, if only because we are a continent, defy rational analysis, whether we consider unemployment among black youths, AIDS, drugs, immigration from Latin America; the list runs on. Emphatically, the North Riding is not Cockaigne. No Roman wall encircles it; it must look out over the North Sea to the continent, and to America across the Atlantic to the west. If the North Riding is pleasantly parochial, that condition can only be temporary. The steadiness and sturdiness of the employed working class contrast with the philistinism of the middle class and the minor aristocracy. England may be the small-talk capital of the world; in many circles, it is considered bad form to mention politics, or civil wars and revolutions in other countries.

To a refugee from "Have a nice day" America, the recent influx into English English of American idiom and slang is a disappointment. Such influence was once deplored, resisted, or very slowly welcomed by the post-Beatles demos. Television and the domination of American films obviously accounts for it, together with the ditching of traditional educational standards at all levels, from primary schools through university. The British suffer from another of our disorders: more books are published each year than in the year preceding, but the identity of the readers is a mystery. In the past, eight out of ten in the London underground read books, according to my personal and unscientific surveys. Now at best it is one in seven; the rest read tabloids or study their shoes. This is all enwrapped in the fog of the 1960s and later anti-élitism, easily detected in the change in announcers' diction from the opulently correct and educated speech of the former BBC men, to a whining pseudo-cockney or regional sing-song of men and women alike. I retired to England to get away from "basically" in every other clause, from "impact" used as a verb, and from "problem," as in "He's got a reading problem." All in vain. The identical abuses are everywhere here, together with native-grown ones: the leader of a local society said of an orchestra, "They augment from London." As in the U.S., the active voice is disappearing. Meanwhile, every word from a foreign language is conscientiously mispronounced. "Nicaragua" rhymes with "what a wag you are," and all French words are accented on the first syllable. George Orwell said that Englishmen believe it to be unmanly to pronounce any foreign word correctly. I have been called pedantic and opinionated, which I am, but I am mollified to find that skimmed (not "skim") milk is not described in scientific percentage of fat, but is "virtually fat-free." A sign on a fish and chip shop announces that, like souls in hell, "We're Frying To-day."

The North Riding, and England beyond it, is not for everyone; it is not instantly palatable, like Córdoba or Verona. If salvation for a district is possible, there may lie its salvation. It resists change: as an officer of the Ridings Society told me, "Napoleon was right when he said that the English are a nation of lions led by donkeys." The district and the country attract me not least because it is not a disgrace, here, to be old. That condescending evasion of ours, "senior citizen" is rare, although it may be heard occasionally. A simple "elderly" is more often used. One result is that the elderly possess a dignity that the American senior citizen in his special leisure clothes often lacks. I have found respect and affection for the old in the North Riding such as I never found in my own country. I think of a conversation with a friend shortly before leaving for England. We had not met for a year or more. When he asked what I was doing, I said that I had retired and was about to sell up and move to England.

"Why are you going to England?"

"The short answer is, there's more time in England. At our age, time matters."

"Yes," he said, "there's more time in England, and there's more love."

I was startled at the directness and the sadness of his remark, but I have often thought of it since, and as often have found it confirmed.

All this does not mean that I am a cultural traitor to my country. I love my country, but it is easier for me to be a good American in England than at home. Assuredly I do not urge an influx of the retired to the North Riding. I would only urge that if one is healthy and lucky enough to be able to choose, it matters to exercise choice rather than have retirement thrust upon one. Re-group, citizens; return to the struggle.

11

Patriots, Expatriates, and Scoundrels

Retirement abroad was prominently in mind as I watched the annual tennis tournament at Wimbledon. They were down to the last sixteen, and the British, who had not turned out champions of late, had grounds for thinking they at last had a man worth supporting. That he was a Canadian with a Slavic surname who claimed to be British did not deter anybody. Desperate for success, they not only waved the Union Jack, they wore it on their heads and painted it on their faces: they were patriots. Their man was playing an American, California-born, of Greek descent, who beat the newly coined Briton in straight sets. I detested the displays in the stands and in the press of what the reporters called patriotism. Yet when the American won, I felt satisfaction, almost a gloat, and hated myself for it.

In a different key from international sport, the idea of patriotism becomes a burning fact in both Europe and world-wide owing to changes in currencies, shifts in economic and political power, and the resulting threats to traditional, almost automatic, unthinking certainties about national sovereignty and personal identity. In the U.S., our size and material dominance, however short-lived it may prove to be, gives us the illusion that our sovereignty and our sense of self is set in concrete. Congress decrees that no one may desecrate the Stars and Stripes. Such patriotism is suspect to many people of more or less open mind who think it is no more than a slogan to urge us to fight wars or to get our votes. Yet the skeptics are also uneasy. They remain aware, however dimly, of innocent, decent, obscurely pastoral connotations of the very word *patriotism*. In my own case, expatriation forced such connotations into prominence, together with an attempt to

129

explain to myself and to my disapproving friends that expatriation could mean enhanced loyalty to my country as ideal and as reality.

Men and women of my time had been educated by experience and theory to distrust all-isms, patriotism foremost. We applauded Samuel Johnson's description of patriotism as "the last refuge of a scoundrel"; but Walter Scott's "Breathes there a man with soul so dead,/ Who never to himself hath said,/ This is my own, my native land!" struck us as comic, and poor poetry to boot. After Ethiopia and Spain, a second world war appeared inevitable, and when it arrived, many of us volunteered stoically, convinced that probably we would not survive. At sea in the Navy, I never heard the word "patriotism" uttered, nor among shipmates any discussion of war aims. In the gray peace and the cold war, patriotism was left to such as Joseph McCarthy, Lyndon Johnson, and Richard Nixon, civilians in uniform who claimed combat experience as witness to their patriotism and to back up their pitch for our votes. John F. Kennedy seemed, for a time, to be the exception; he was a man of various distinctions, and for a politician, he did not prate extravagantly. Until the Bay of Pigs adventure, his "Ask not what your country can do for you, but what you can do for your country" appeared to be the nearest tolerable appeal to patriotism.

In my reaction to a tennis match, as in Samuel Johnson's and Walter Scott's contradictory attitudes to patriotism lay a slippery concept, one involving memory, experience, and a long, tangled history. One can bear only so much ambiguity. The central ambiguity seemed to relate to the point at which a benevolent emotion, patriotism, slid over into a fanatical, murderous drive: nationalism. Historical event, as is usual, overtook and twisted etymology. In ancient Greek, *pater, patriotes* (father, of one's father) and their Latin counterparts referred to the immediate family, to the home, hearth and soil, the *patria*. As pastoral, agricultural, and religious, limited to daily human and animal encounters and to animistic gods all but tangible, *patria* constituted a Good in national memory, allied, no doubt, to the recurring myth of a Golden Age. In iron reality, the emotions of *patria* were also xenophobic, justifying war on barbarians, the killing or enslaving of the defeated in the name of one's own tribe, and supported by sacrifices to one's own gods. The Trojan war was tribal rather than national: its immediate cause, the seizure of Helen by Paris, was an offense to Menelaus, not to a nonexistent Greek nation. It is the gods, not national flags, that preside over the battles on the Trojan plain.

With the foundation of the city-states, the abstraction of the State came into being (later to be sanctified by Hegel), an entity to which the citizen owed his loyalty and if necessary his life in combat against enemies. In literature the Horatian *dulce et decorum est pro patria mori,* and the militant Virgilian *arma virumque cano* displaced the bucolic eclogues and georgics. By the time of World War I, such sentiments had descended, or ascended, to the U.S. Marine sergeant's urging his platoon over the top: "Let's go, you sons of bitches, do you want to live forever?" Both Plato in *The Republic,* and Aristotle asserted the precedence of the State over the individual, just as Jews and Greeks maintained a "racial nationalism,"[1] Hans Kohn remarks. As for the Roman Empire, the announced ideal of *pax et justicia* was attained only briefly, but in it we may see a genuine attempt to tame the malevolence of the idea of the State into the pastoral virtues of Virgilian eclogue, and in Virgil's epithet, *pius Aeneas* for the hero of his epic poem.

These matters are not confined to the West. In c. 1050 A.D., the Islamic scholar Alberuni wrote of the Hindus that they "'believe that there is no country but theirs, no nation like theirs. They are haughty, foolishly vain, self-conceited, and stolid. They are by nature niggardly in communicating what which they know, and they take the greatest possible care to withhold it from men of another caste among their own people, still much more, of course, from any foreigner.'"[2]

Patriotism, then, is at once a deep, and at bottom, decent emotion, to which humanity West and East has been tempted repeatedly and tragically to attach increasingly dubious political and sociological interpretations. Patriotism lost its last vestige of innocence in the aftermath of the French Revolution. Romantic epistemology and aesthetics, opposed to the cosmopolitanism and Cartesian rationalism of the Enlightenment, stressed the new psychology of individualism. The Napoleonic conquests, in turn, gave political substance to the new philosophy in the form of national states and the accompanying ideology of the State. A tribal, subliminal memory of a benevolent *patria* became *la patrie* to the tune of "La Marseillaise," or *Vaterland* to the

---

1. Hans Kohn, *The Idea of Nationalism* (New York: Collier Books, 1967 [1st. ed. 1944], p. 19.
2. Quoted in Niran C. Chaudhuri, *The Autobiography of an Unknown Indian* (London: Macmillan, 1951), p. 409.

tune of "Deutschland über Alles." Hence reverence for a benign locality became blurred, the shift in meaning as distinct as peace and war, health and sickness. In the process, cynics and the naive among politicians, journalists, bishops, generals, admirals, judges, and professors knowingly or unknowingly were in collusion.

Chamber's Dictionary defines "patriot" as "one who truly, though sometimes injudiciously, loves and serves his fatherland." J.H. Grainger nicely defined nationalism as "the old *patria* overwhelmed with doctrine." He writes further that nationalism is active and thrusting, a constant arousal to national consciousness. Patriotism and nationalism became hopelessly entangled in the various episodes of national expansion: the British in India in the eighteenth century; the Napoleonic conquests, opposition to which aroused national fervor throughout Europe; the white American drives through the native Indian lands, to French Louisiana, Mexico, Alaska, the Philippines and to Panama. Such expansions created prosperity, or its illusion, for the invaders; with the increased sense of national triumph came not so much identity as national egotisms leading to smouldering and persistent enmities. If the citizen could not go out to slaughter the lesser breeds in the name of the nation, at home there was the seductive flag-waving as a substitute for thought, the conviction of pride that one's own kind were now proved superior to all rivals. Xenophobia took the place of Enlightenment cosmopolitanism, and of the fond false memory of unity imposed by the mediaeval church and by the Holy Roman Empire.

After Napoleon, the French, and the Germans under Bismarck specialized in patriotism. In 1916, in the face of unparalleled slaughter, the historian Alphonse Aulard could write:

> Truth fights eternally for France. The German sacrifices himself to a material ideal. The Frenchman dies for the true ideal, the living ideal, and as his *patrie* is constructed on the very same ideal, the more patriotic he is, the more he serves truth, the future, humanity. Our men sacrifice themselves as intelligent heroes, entering in full knowledge into the highest glory, with a pleasure very French in being right. The German cannot have the same degree of will, impregnated as he is with error, a slave of the past. The French republic no longer merely announces the rights of man; she defends them with good 75's, with good machine guns, with good mortars loaded with solid steel, and by killing as many Germans as possible. She still has not killed enough of them.[3]

---

3. J.H. Grainger, *Patriotisms: Britain, 1900–1939* (London: Routledge & Kegan Paul, 1986).

Patriotism joined to hysteria, nationalism, and bloodthirsty xenophobia here mingle in logical progression, but masked as wartime moral philosophy. On the German side, Thomas Mann sounded a similar note in 1914, writing that Germans were fighting against a civilization gone bad, that war would reinvigorate a country dulled by peace. (Mann's genius, as I read him, was to find himself on the right side, and at the right time, of all questions.)

For roughly a century in the United States—from, say, 1850 to 1950—two distinct conditions affected our sense of nationality: the Civil War, which imposed and enforced national unity, and in another idiom, modern psychology, which analyzed our special nervousness about the national condition and gave us what soon became cant—concern for personal identity, together with a parallel concern for national identity. In our pseudo-psychological culture, the young are encouraged to "find" themselves, thus assuming that they are already lost. Mass immigration has marked us indelibly since the mid-nineteenth century. In the succeeding waves of immigration of Germans, Irish, Poles, Jews, Hungarians, Italians, the immigrant (Chinese excepted) was the first to take on the attributes of the American. The new Americans abandoned their mother-tongue, learned English, and sent the children to English-language schools. They waved the flag more vigorously than the native and the men cheerfully volunteered to fight in our wars. The immigrants became assimilated, in brief, and soon aspired to, and gained, political power.

Broadly sketched, such was the portrait until the end of World War II. The long overdue emergence of the Southern (and often the Northern) blacks to some kind of political equality with whites would result in a profound departure from our former nationalist axioms. Large numbers of blacks did not so much accept previous nationalist views, as draw apart from them in a manner unsettling to the tried and true white patriot. Post-World War II migrations of Puerto Ricans to mainland cities, the influx of Asians, together with immigration, mainly illegal, from Latin America have changed patterns of language, education, economics, and politics unrecognizably to Americans of earlier vintage. These are matters of fact, recognized as such by liberals and conservatives alike. What may be recognized but not admitted is that the successive waves of upheaval resulting from these movements of populations have challenged and stretched our traditional assumptions about the very existence of patriotic impulses and behavior.

Over a meal with an old friend visiting England from Boston, the subject of patriotism versus expatriation came up. My friend, who had fought willingly and well in World War II, remarked about a U.S. Marine atrocity in Vietnam, "After My Lai, I could never again call myself a patriot." Increasingly it became admitted that our adventures in Vietnam from the early 1960s to the fall of Saigon in 1975, actions that filled the graveyards with war dead and over-filled the veterans' hospitals with the maimed, tested our sense of patriotism as no previous events had done. That undeclared war damaged us so irrevocably because it was fought mainly by an "underclass" (translation: poor bastards) who either volunteered their way out of poverty, as they had always done, feeling a glow of patriotism; or they were conscripted for lack of middle-class recourses, such as physicians' certificates of neurosis, or a suddenly discovered need for uninterrupted "higher" education. With the publicity given to the nastiness of that war, exacerbated no doubt by the troops' reported intake of drugs, the American public learned how foul things were, events culminating in the intolerable fact that our forces had been defeated by a bunch of pajama-clad guerillas armed with little more than firecrackers. As the ex-volunteers and conscripts returned to their *patria* they promptly learned that what their countrymen recalled were not the heroic actions for which President Johnson had so liberally handed out Congressional Medals of Honor, but troops battering peasants with rifle butts, the destruction of ancient farming lands, the living, burning bodies of Asian children. Apart from a handful of self-serving generals, few in the population were tempted to call Vietnam a "good" war, as we believed we had been able to call World War II a "good" war.

Such a history may suggest that in the United States a non-fascistic, uncynical order of patriotism requires unquestioning blind faith, as does religion. Not many of us are saints, and only unthinking optimism linked to historical ignorance now produces patriots, it appears.

If not patriots, what then about expatriates? For Americans, expatriation has usually been tainted, suggesting if not treason, undue and unjustified self-reliance, together with contempt for those of their countrymen who make their peace with the realities, pleasant and unpleasant, of their birthplace. Dictionary definitions of expatriation are less than helpful, for they emphasize exile and banishment, as well as voluntary departure from one's homeland. As used here, "expatriation" applies only to one voluntarily choosing to live for an indefinite period in a country other than that of one's birth. It does not apply to people posted abroad by businesses or government, nor to travelers who prolong a temporary residence abroad. It does not apply to refugees or exiles, those forced to leave as punishment or under other duress. The essence of expatriation as commonly understood now is that it is voluntary. To the homebound it often appears that in the act of choice, the expatriate spurns the *patria* from spite, to escape the sheriff, Internal Revenue agents, or from some other dubious motive. Expatriation may mean a new language or an oblique usage of one's own language; our writers therefore are our best witnesses when such slippery terms come into question.

The poet, Elizabeth Bishop wrote to a friend from Paris in 1935: "I am not, never never an **expatriate**. We went to tea at Comtesse de Chambrun's and I met a few men—so languid, so whimsical, so *cultured*—youthfully middle-aged, and remind me of nothing so much as a flourishing fuzzy gray *mold*." She wrote this long before her nineteen years of expatriation near Petrópolis, Brazil, to be sure; but the sentiment from that very American poet also represents, I believe, the response of a significant range of American characters in Henry James's fiction. Our most noted literary expatriates: James, Gertrude Stein, Ezra Pound, T.S. Eliot, and Ernest Hemingway had in common one characteristic. They were all born into what they considered a cultural desert, and each, more steeped than he perhaps knew by his *tierra,* his *patria,* left for Europe, where in varying degrees his literary ambitions were fulfilled.

Henry James's Cambridge as he describes it in *The Bostonians,* for example, is a poor place of muddy streets and cheap frame houses, but not the cultural center it prided itself on being. James's famous lament about America bears quotation here: "no annals for the historian, no follies (beyond the most vulgar and commonplace) for the satirist; no manners for the dramatist; no obscure fictions for the writer of romance; no gross and hardy offences against decorum for the moralist; nor any of the rich, artificial auxiliaries of poetry. . . . I have never seen a nation so alike in my life, as the people of the United States, and what is more, they are not only like each other, but they are remarkably like that which common sense tells them they ought to resemble. . . . There is no costume for the peasant (there is scarcely a peasant at all), no wig for the judge, no baton for the general, no diadem for the chief magistrate." Returning to America after twenty-one years abroad, James found little reason to alter his earlier view of the country. In *The American Scene* (1904–1905), James regrets the "unfinished" character of the country, manners so indiscriminate that there could not be "any manners to speak of"; he deplores our "large mistrust of privacy" accompanied by a dominant commercial spirit: "gold-dust in the air." "As the usual, in our cast crude democracy of trade, is the new, the simple, the cheap, the common, the commercial, the immediate, and, all too often, the ugly." By the end of his travels, his major complaint stands out as it had in his earlier lament: our "repudiation of the past." James's vehemence may be seen to betray a lack of profound knowledge of his country, together with the hurt of a scorned lover when considering a once-beloved.

Neither Gertrude Stein's native California nor study in psychology with William James at Radcliffe tempted her to remain in the East or to return to the West, no more tempting to her than Idaho had been to Ezra Pound. Both lived out their lives abroad, as would Eliot. Ultimately Hemingway returned by way of Cuba not to suburban Oak Park, Illinois, but to Montana, where he shot game birds, and finally himself.

It is in James's career, as in the careers of other writers and painters foremost, that the advantages and the difficulties of expatriation emerge most clearly. An entire industry has been given over to analysis of James's American abroad, his major theme: the disparity between charming but provincial American origins and the presumed superiority of the European scene, English or continental. Again and again in his fiction, James's imagination calls for the foreign scene as only an expatriate is likely to do, as an evocation not of a remembered America, but one colored by an unescapably American palette. In *The Tragic Muse* (1890) the young Englishman, Nick Dormer, newly elected to Parliament, strolls through the grounds of Beauclere Abbey on a summer's day. His spirit, James writes, is tempted to sink into the "tide of time" that

> broke with a ripple too faint to be a warning. . . . The light lingered on the rough red walls and the local accent of the children sounded soft in the church-yard. It was simply the sense of England—a sort of apprehended revelation of his country. The dim annals of the place were sensibly, heavily in the air—foundations bafflingly early, a great monastic life, wars of the Roses, with battles and blood in the streets, and the long quietude of the respectable centuries, all corn-fields and magistrates and vicars—and these things were connected with an emotion that arose from the green country, the rich land so infinitely lived in, and laid on him a hand that too

ghostly to press and yet somehow too urgent to be light. . . . These impressions melted together and made a general appeal, of which, with his new honours as a legislator, he was the sentient subject. If he had a love for that particular scene of life mightn't it have a love for him and expect something of him? What fate could be so high as to grow old in a national affection? What a fine sort of reciprocity, making mere soreness of all the balms of indifference!

I doubt that any English writer could have given Nick Dormer the particular historical awareness, or lack thereof, that James here depicts. As a well-brought-up child Nick would have been subjected to relentless drill in prep school and public school concerning early history; nor would the Roman Catholic monastic past have been judged "great" (in James's sense) after the Reformation. As for "the long quietude of the respectable centuries," Nick Dormer's history masters long before would have expounded on factional disputes, the many wars, and the revolution of 1688. James's history is the product not of reading and research, but of his insistence in many of his writings on the grubbiness of the American past in contrast to his sanitized versions of the British and European past. His version of nature in England, like Proust's version of nature in Normandy, is equally idealized. Fine summer days are the rule, rain is rare, the winds never howl, and lightning never strikes.

James reveals a characteristic example of the expatriate's mind, in which partial memory of the native country combines with an oblique view of the adopted scene; an interior dispute takes place, productive for the writer but never really resolved. James's long residence in England, culminating in British citizenship one year before his death in 1916, did not and could not make him English, any more than T.S. Eliot's career made him English. We have only to recall Virginia Woolf's nasty comment in *A Writer's Diary* on *The Wings of the Dove:* "Not a flabby or slack sentence, but much emasculated by this timidity or consciousness or whatever it is. Very highly American, I conjecture, in the determination to be highly bred, and the light obtuseness as to what high breeding is." Just as Quentin Anderson could write a study called *The American Henry James,* an investigation of James's enduring American sensibility, so with profit might someone write a similar study of Eliot's work. Neither Savile Row tailoring, nor Eliot's self-proclaimed royalism and Anglicanism could eliminate family, St. Louis, Missouri, and an American education. You can go native but never arrive.

Hemingway's best work might seem remote from James's, but both expatriated writers repeatedly indicate a sensibility formed in America and only slightly transformed by the foreign scene. Compare the short story, "Big, Two-Hearted River" with the idyllic trout-fishing episode in Navarre in Hemingway's first novel, *The Sun Also Rises.* In each narrative, respect for fact in nature, carefully observed, combines with understated or unstated joy in the natural setting. No Spaniard has perceived a Spanish scene like Hemingway's: Pío Baroja, for one, describes similar northern Spanish landscapes, but the result is remote from Hemingway's, not in quality but in selection and apprehension and emotion. Hemingway learned a great deal from James: unspoken responses, and an undertow of tragedy, but he seasoned his lessons with diction learned in part from Mark Twain. That diction served him well in his early and best work; it failed him, I think, when his narratives took him into the minds of Spanish characters in *For Whom the Bell Tolls,* or to the old man of *The Old Man and the Sea.* A roaming expatriate in France, Spain, Africa, Cuba, Hemingway remained irrevocably American, a cosmopolite in a baseball cap.

Ezra Pound's relationship to the United States is like that of a man who both loves and beats his wife. No matter how remote his distance from his first country, in his very hectoring of American poets and editors, as well as in his rhythms, his themes in the *Cantos,* and in his diction, a betrayed love for his country cannot be hidden by all his excoriation of it, however dressed in aesthetic and economic terms. He would out-Dante Dante, import Chinese wisdom with what he believed to be the hard concreteness of Chinese characters into verse laden with American slang and ironic cliché. Through it all, even in his broadcasts from Rome during World War II, throughout his correspondence even after his commitment to a psychiatric hospital, his language retains an American vigor, a looniness such as we also find in Marianne Moore, William Carlos Williams, or E.E. Cummings. It lodges in spontaneous non-logical jumps that nevertheless are wittily right; it is free, and earnest without being leaden. It is not English and not European, and it gives Pound his indubitable Americanness even as he aspires to far-flung internationalism. It accounts for his infrequent successes, but it weakens those parts of the *Cantos* built on mere pastiche: entire lengthy passages that I, for one, find stagy and bogus.

The fact that Ezra Pound was captured by the American army in Italy, declared a traitor for his wartime broadcasts from Rome, and imprisoned in a cage like an animal in a zoo may symbolize a common attitude toward the expatriate: he appears as a traitor to all the patriot holds dear; by the action of removing himself he denies the uniqueness, the greatness of his native soil. I think again to Berlin in the 1950s and to the contempt directed to those who had been forced out but who chose to return to try to resume their German lives.

If the idea of expatriation makes the true-blue patriot uneasy, the idea of the cosmopolitan may make him even more so: in an assessment of John Singer Sargent's character and work, an American magazine writer refers to "the odd, lunar isolation of Americans abroad,"[4] a typical statement issuing from that insular U.S. province, New York City. At issue in all the foregoing is the barrier between the seductive nationalism that would encompass the true patriot, and the rootless cosmopolitan who owes allegiance to the gods know what or to whom. When asked where his *patria* was, Anaxagoras pointed to the sky, and Seneca said his was *totus mundus*, the whole world. Cosmopolitans make poor foot-soldiers. Consistent with the neo-classical and Englightenment outlook, cosmopoltanism was a noble ideal, one pursued in philosophy and the arts, if not in military adventures. With the explosion of nineteenth-century nationalism, the cosmopolitan was seen with suspicion, if not contempt. Conservatives in politics always looked down on socialists as contemptible cosmopolitans, while anti-Semites saw the Jews as cosmopolites, therefore unpatriotic, rootless, and lacking national identity.

The assertion of national identity is attractive to politicians, for it allows them a flattering appeal to national uniqueness, and however specious, to superiority, an inevitable recourse in time of war or threats of war. At its most paltry, nationalism is mere local boosterism; at its best, it may foster great art in mysterious ways: I think of Wagner. At its most dangerous, it results in holocausts. Within the easy appeal of nationalism lies a snarled ball of assumptions: that one's culture is rooted in language and expressed in customs and habits with twists of meaning unknown to and incapable of comprehension by other national entities. In its most desperate forms, such assertions of uniqueness lead to the rewriting of history and denial of tangible facts of experience, as twentieth-century history so unpleasantly has shown us. It is therefore strange to find an intellectual cosmopolitan such as

---

4.   Adam Gopnik, "Sargent's Pearls," *The New Yorker* (February 15, 1999), 66.

Isaiah Berlin writing that "cosmopolitanism is the shedding of all that makes one most human, most oneself." Berlin, born in what was Imperial Russia, became a Fellow of All Souls, Oxford, holder of the Order of Merit, recipient of many other honors, was ardently British and a Zionist, a cosmopoitan, one might think, who abjured his own biography in the service of an emotional conviction. "A sane nationalism," he said, "is to be justified by a utilitarian argument—that most men and women are happy only when their way of life prolongs customs and habits which are familiar to them."

Now, however, nationalism seems recessive, and an internet cosmopolitanism appears dominant. We deplore nationalism in the Balkans; commerce increasingly becomes international. Europeans adopt a single currency, while the United States hopes for economic bliss in Free Trade. Norwegians and Tibetans sing country-and-western lyrics, as jeans and T-shirts rule the day, the decade, the generations. All that, however, may be only a cheap patina over a thick layer of residual nationalism. The expatriate apparently is a cosmopolitan of a peculiarly guilty sort. In colloquial German, *ein Kosmopolit* is a well-dressed fraud who sits about in cafés affecting insouciance.

I suspect that the expatriate is less likely to be insouciant than the local patriot—and to be more genuinely patriotic. To exercise choice, as the expatriate by definition has done, is liberating. Comparisons need not be odious, and the expatriate perceives his country as the homebound cannot, an assertion that would deny Henry James's words concerning the expatriated American sculptor, William Wetmore Story: "a man always pays, in one way or another, for expatriation, for detachment from his plain primary heritage." One may also pay for remaining bogged down in his plain primary heritage. Expatriation is a voyage from two dimensions into three. In living among the strong and the weak points of a foreign culture, one discovers that the virtues and strengths of one's *patria* stand out boldly. At home, besieged by the flow of ephemera communicated moment by moment, all becomes flat and two-dimensional. Prolonged residence abroad tests and reinforces the expatriate's loyalty to homeland and to its language and customs.

At home I am hourly, daily, indignant at our failures and muffed opportunities. Abroad I defend, explain, and forgive. I become a patriotic expatriate. W.H. Auden, from 1939 an English expatriate in the United States, remarked in an address to the Grolier Club in 1947:

"Those who become expatriates out of hatred for their homeland are as bound to the past as those who hate their parents." But he also said in the same address, "You must leave your country to love it." I find Auden correct in both remarks, but when Wimbledon comes round again, I shall not be painting an American flag on my face.

12

Notes on a War

You shipped him off address unknown
You shipped him far beyond Endurance
I cannot reach him on the phone
He left me all his life insurance.

"Elegy"

This pig, the World, is roasted on a spit;

"Vilanelle"

—William Jay Smith, Collected Poems: 1939–
1989

October, 1998. For the better part of a year, my friend Shaw's fifty-six-foot sloop lay up in a boatyard for modifications, at Lorient, Brittany, on the Bay of Biscay. Now, the work completed, three of us had assembled for a leisurely shakedown cruise to the ancient and unbombed port of La Rochelle, Charente-Maritime.

I had never been to Lorient before, but I knew its notoriety as the first major base in France for German U-boats in World War II ("my" war), and nearby Kernaval as headquarters of Admiral Dönitz, director of U-boat operations, and in 1945 successor to Hitler. I was eager to see the U-boat pens of Lorient, and not more than a mile from our mooring, there they loomed. By the time we had installed provisions and settled in aboard, it was late of a quiet Sunday afternoon. Virtually without discussion, we agreed that a trip in the inflatable dinghy to look over the U-boat pens had to be made. I knew that the pens had been constructed with slave-labor in 1941 by the same contractors who had built the German U-Bahns, and that American commentators had criticized the British for bombing the site only sporadically before the pens had been completed. The British, to be sure, had the Blitz to contend with.

Proceeding under outboard motor past the fishermen's docks, we came up slowly on the monsters, high over us, at water level. Our word "pen," suggesting sheep or rabbits, does justice neither to the German *Bunkeranlage* nor to the lowering massiveness of the elephant-gray concrete structures rising ever higher above us as we approached. No more than 300 yards distant from the central bunker lies the rusting wreck of a U-boat that was bombed and sunk in the shallows in 1944, within spitting distance of home. In line with the sunken U-boat we could make out the sunken hull of a freighter, its superstructure resembling a gun emplacement, but now a roost for hundreds of gulls. The ship had been sunk by the Allies to bottle up the boats[1] then in the bunkers for repairs.

Moving slowly along the entrances to the bunkers, some protected by guillotine-like gates, even the uninterruptedly garrulous Shepherd, the third of our crew, fell silent at the eighty-foot high caverns within, roofs and walls made of twelve feet of reinforced concrete, dark in the early evening sunlight, silent, Wagnerian. Two gates had rusted away; others hung obliquely useless. Each bunker, some 400 yards long, had accommodated two submarines, with the exception of the last, which was twice as wide as the others, with capacity for four boats. Defying posted signs, *defendu* "by military order," Shaw steered the dinghy into the cavern, where at the far end we could just make out the remains of an underwater railway for hauling boats up into dry-dock. In the gloom, it looked like a stage, bearing out the Wagnerian effect, but only an operatic silence, rusting reinforcement rods and rotting concrete overhead provided the décor for this *Götterdämmerung*. I was frankly relieved when we emerged without having been bashed by falling concrete, great hunks of which hung at unlikely angles from bent reinforcement rods. We agreed it was no wonder that with the loss of so many Allied planes and men over these bunkers, no amount of bombing could have put them out of action; not even the 4,500 tons of bombs they had sustained by 1943 alone. As we moved away, I

---

1. In naval parlance, submarines are "boats" despite their size and capacity. All other ocean-going vessels are "ships."

counted six gun anti-aircraft gun emplacements on top of the bunkers, and later we found the sites ashore of many more in the vicinity of the bunkers. Although the bombs had done no detectable damage to the bunkers, the bombers had succeeded in wiping out the ancient city of Lorient. I thought of the Japanese bunkers on Tarawa: huge bamboo constructions, eighteen feet deep, that neither bombs nor sixteen-inch naval shells had damaged before the Marines invaded in November, 1943.

Neither of my middle-aged companions had been old enough to serve in the Second World War; they saw the bunkers in a perspective different from mine. I had spent five years in the U.S. Navy, in anti-submarine warfare. Those haunting bunkers at Lorient retrieved emotions and events of half a century earlier, things I had thought to be safely sequestered wherever in our consciousness we try to dispose of such matters.

Near the end of our training as officers and gentlemen, my roommate and friend (the one rarely implies the other), William Jay Smith, and I volunteered for duty in bomb-disposal. We had been lured by a recruiter's description of the bomb-disposal officer's duties and perquisites: a cabin to himself in a battleship or cruiser; relatively few shipboard duties, and, we deduced, plenty of time for writing, given the odds against an unexploded bomb at sea. We could simultaneously serve our country and serve ourselves: what more could a man ask in time of war? Bill Smith had already published some of the poetry that was to make him known and honored; I merely aspired to write. Fortunately we were both turned down for bomb disposal. Neither of us was particularly gifted mechanically, and confronted with defusing an unexploded bomb, without any doubt we would have blown it, our shipmates, and ourselves sky high.

Since an existence of patriotic hedonism aboard a battleship was denied to me, I put in for destroyer duty. Destroyers had style. They were dashing, versatile, and the source of many a great naval career. I had no ambitions for a naval career or any other conventional career, however. Conditioned by a semi-military childhood and my reading, I felt certain that I would not survive the war, like many another man of my time. Such romantic, doom-laden thoughts, in my case at least, were a form of cowardice, escape-devices: escape from uncertain plans in a hypothetical, postwar future. I think it is this that attracts many, if not most men to warfare. For us, it was not that we wanted to go out to maim and kill, but for a time to be free from the mundane responsibilities, the grinding realities of earning a living, and the dispiriting civilian competition for place and esteem. To a seagoing man a destroyer was the equivalent of a pursuit plane to men attracted to aviation. If I was to go down to feed the fish, I would go down in style. As for attitudes to war, I think of V.S. Naipaul, a man who fought in no war, who writes about "spirituality" in war, describing how in the eight-year-long Iran-Iraq war, a boy-soldier of thirteen strapped a bomb to himself, threw himself beneath an Iraqi tank, so blowing up it and himself, and becoming the most famous official martyr of the war. Naipaul also writes of the "spirituality" of a fourteen-year old in the Martyrs Battalion who each evening would go to the morgue near the battlefield, collect the equipment of the dead and wash it for reissue.[2] Naipaul is describing fanaticism, to be sure, but his attitude could be seen as a pitch to support pacifism. We were neither fanatics nor pacifists; we were resigned, and curious to know what our fate would offer.

Few of any of us non-Annapolis, newly created ensigns of the Naval Reserve were sent to destroyers at that point in the war. Many, including me, got orders to a new order of ship with a destroyer's handsome lines, but one-third her dimensions. Desperate for convoy escorts, President Roosevelt chose to ignore senior naval advice that we build more destroyers in favor of a ship that could be produced fast and in quantity, one designed specifically for anti-submarine warfare. Small, at 173 feet in length, eighteen feet in the beam, the PC class was not honored with names but with numbers, like streets in Manhattan; token of the professional navy's contempt for anything less than destroyers. Shallow in draft, therefore an unlikely target for a torpedo, the PC was more maneuverable than a destroyer; equipped with the latest echo-sounding gear (Sonar), a 3"50 calibre gun forward, a 40 millimeter gun aft, numerous 20 millimeter Oerlikon anti-aircraft guns, Y-guns and depth charge racks, the PC could more than hold its own against submarines, fend off air attack if lucky, and relieve destroyers, with their greater range and heavier armament, for more exigent tasks with the Fleet.

Allied (and some neutral) losses to Axis U-boats in 1939–1942 had

---

2. V.S. Naipaul, *Beyond Belief: Islamic Excursions among the Converted Peoples* (London: Little, Brown and Company. 1998), p. 151, p. 203.

been nearly catastrophic: 1,124 ships, including twenty-eight warships, of some 5.3 million gross tons, had gone to the bottom, and thousands of men who manned those ships had been killed.[3] By late 1942, despite having lost twenty-one U-boats and 1,000 of his most experienced men during 1941–1942, Dönitz had been able to send to sea twenty boats a month in the Atlantic, Caribbean, and South American waters by mid-1942. Such was German production at that point, and such was the threat to our shipping as my ship put to sea after some scanty anti-aircraft training and surface target practice off the Virginia coast, and brief, essential sea-trials of the twin-diesel engines.

Our orders were to shake down while proceeding to Miami for further training, but at the last moment we were sent to rendezvous with an incoming convoy 100 miles into the Atlantic off Delaware, to relieve one of the escorts, and to proceed with the convoy to New York. In the event, none of that happened. Winters, our commanding officer, was a Regular Navy lieutenant-commander, an engineering officer by training, who owing to peacetime lack of money for the Navy, had hardly ever been to sea, and had rarely conned a ship. Lieutenant (junior grade) U.S. Naval Reserve Hutton, the executive officer, had joined the reserve training unit at Yale, but he had never been to sea, beyond a midshipman cruise, and very soon became so seasick as to be useless. Among the three ensigns, only I had been to sea, if only for a few months. Winters and I, together with our handful of Regular Navy petty officers remained healthy, but the green crewmen were in bad shape. Denver, the boatswain, complained that half of them were "too stupid to vomit to leeward."

The weather was foul, the seas moderate but rough enough to look hostile to the unaccustomed. It turned cold, and spray soaked the watch on deck. We had not drawn North Atlantic foul-weather gear, for we had been on our way to the tropics. Two hours out of port, the green-faced exec, also in theory the navigator, confessed that he had no confidence in his dead-reckoning plot and could produce only an approximate idea of our position. Some hours after nightfall, we signaled a passing aircraft: "What is my position?" We proved to be thirty miles off the point of rendezvous; about midnight coded orders came to proceed to Miami for final anti-sub warfare training, as origi-

---

3. Clay Blair, Hitler's U-boat War: 1939–1942 (New York: Random House, 1996, 1998), two vols. Vol I, p. 418, and Appendix 17.

nally directed. The first day of our maiden voyage had been a *pachanga:* Mexican for a state of total chaos.

The official complement of the PC class was six officers and some seventy men, but I knew no ship that ever had more than five officers and about sixty-five men. In space so confined, it was essential that all hands got on well, but given our human/animal nature, that proved other-worldly. Hutton bothered me no end. I felt sorry for him, in one way, because obviously he was not up to the job, nor was he cut out to be a seaman. He seemed never to recover from his loss of face during our first venture out of the shipyard. He concealed shame by snappishness, and by what I took for snobbery. Socially uncertain myself and quick to take offence, I thought that Hutton regarded me and the other ensigns as social inferiors, jumped-up hicks from second-rate state universities. I considered Hutton to be the essential, anti-intellectual bourgeois, literally at sea now and suffering from the shock of his new milieu: ours was not the ceremonial sword-carrying shore navy of his Yale unit. I was fully aware of my own hypocrisy. If I really identified myself with the working class, I should have been a deck hand, but I told myself that I had already been through that and had earned the right to sneer at such as Lt.(j.g.) Hutton.

In contrast, Winters, grandson of an admiral and son of a captain, was totally at ease, if not in charge, in any and all situations. A man of great charm, and wonderfully open about himself and his experience, he kept the wardroom in a truce, if not at full peace, while some of his habits and attitudes instructed me valuably in how (and how not) to run a command. He knew Spanish well and had a literary turn, unusual in what I would encounter among regular Navy officers. Despite his lapses, the men respected him for his understanding when they got in trouble ashore, and for his willingness to listen and to learn from the petty officers. I liked him and had the illusion that he liked me.

"I never wanted to go to the Academy," he told me one evening in the Officers' Club at Guantanamo Bay. "I went automatically, because my family took it for granted. I was to be the fourth generation of naval officers. As simple as that." He ordered another drink. "My best subject at the Academy was Spanish."

Winters was in his early forties, I gathered. Married with two children, he had found the Navy a pleasant, secure trap during the Depression. Now his classmates at Annapolis were commanders or executive officers in destroyers, or division commanders on battleships. Without whining about it, Winters implied that he knew he was failing in his profession by having been ordered to a mere PC, and he continued from long habit to drink himself unconscious at every opportunity. Whenever we touched port, he would detail Hutton to attend the usual convoy conference, then sprint for the officers' club bar, or any other bar if we had not put in to a naval base. These occasions were few and limited in time, but our captain would have to be half-carried back to the ship and poured into his bunk, sometimes by the petty officer of the deck. Safely out to sea and on station, patrolling our sector of the convoy, Winters would need a day or two of silence before returning to his genial, humorous self.

Safely at sea was not always the case. On our third Cuba-Trinidad-Cuba run, we had some twelve hours at Guantanamo to lay in ammunition, fuel, and provisions before sailing at 0500. Winters was still unsteady and glassy-eyed when he arrived on deck to con the ship out of the slip.

"Shall I take the con, captain?" Hutton reasonably suggested.

"I'll con my own ship. Let go all lines."

"All lines clear, sir," the bridge talker reported.

"All engines back full."

It was an unfortunate command. We shot out of the slip like a stone from a sling, ending up high on a mud bank, propellers racing in the airy void. Winters must have believed he was back in a destroyer with steam engines requiring full power to get underway, unlike our diesels. A commanding officer in the Naval Reserve would have been court-martialed for beaching his ship, but the Regular Navy looked after its own. A tug arrived to tow us off, we caught up with our convoy, and no more was heard of the event.

Everyone I had known, everyone I met in the navy, enlisted men and officers alike drank too much whenever they had the chance. Since we were at sea most of the time, opportunities were rare; unlike the British Navy, our ships had been dry since 1919, hence drink became all the more a longed-for solace. I was no exception, but the image of our ship on that Cuban mud bank remained in my mind and kept me from excessive excess. That other solace, women, were scarcer than drink. Some of the men patronized bordellos when time, place, and liberty allowed; officers, many of whom had recently been married, combined fidelity with fear of venereal infection to remain chaste, making do with strong drink. By 1945, one of the men in my ship computed, ruefully, that we had seen just one woman in eighteen months, and she a crone on one of the islands of Kwajalein Atoll.

Seagoing officers' prophylactic delicacy with respect to whores raised the whole issue of class in my mind, both in and out of the Navy. As I have noted previously, my own origins were proletarian and low middle class; I had gravitated toward the radical politics of the 1930s, for there was no other place for people like me. I felt contempt for men who had not worked hard with their hands, even while I struggled to get away from continuing to work hard with *my* hands. My tastes were literary and foppish, and as I have also noted, people with whom I did manual labor would complain that I did not look like a working man, their comment lying somewhere between disparaging and complimentary; I chose to accept it as the latter. Having chosen to become an officer, I had betrayed my class and my always lukewarm radical politics. I preferred an officer's uniform to the slightly ridiculous eighteenth-century rig of the enlisted seaman, although I found most officers' company predicable, anti-intellectual and dull. The sailors were more interesting in their speech and in their excesses. When an image of Billy Budd, a blond, blue-eyed innocent from the prairies was assigned to my first command, the regulars told him in our first liberty port that he wasn't in the navy until he had been "stewed, screwed, and tattooed." In the morning he awoke somewhere in Havana with an aching head and a large Donald Duck tattooed on his chest. I compared the crew I had known aboard the tanker *Guadalajara* in 1936; we had never been able to buy more than a beer and a cheap meal ashore.

In Winters's ship my position was untenable, even insufferable, but I found low pleasure in closing my volume of Proust to recall to my middle-class fellow officers my membership in the Hod Carriers Union, A. F. of L. When wardroom talk for the nth time was about meals in a fraternity house at the University of X, I would describe the cuisine aboard a boxcar somewhere between Kansas City and Nowhere. They should have pushed me over the side on a dark night. It must be said that the Navy gave people like me a code of conduct, far from contemptible in itself; a special language, a prescribed form of dress, and automatic status, temporary to be sure. We were actors in a play in which the speeches had been written for us, but a play having a beginning but no middle or end, as year after year the war dragged on. I had learned deportment, social and intellectual, from the nuns in grade school, from a handful of admired teachers, and from reading books.

Such training was valuable, but it did not create confidence or provide social practice; thus the naval, gentlemanly codes, often breached rather than observed by some, were a relief from doubts for me. I could get on with the task in hand. Nevertheless, for many years I had regarded the wealthy and the well-born with a corrosive mixture of contempt and envy.[4] At age twenty, I did not realize how very American I was in such matters.

I was ambitious (only the wealthy can afford not to be), but I was not a good team man. I had to struggle against an impulse to push Christiansen, communications officer, over the side. A Texan oaf, he had got his commission through an uncle in Texas politics. Overweight and out of shape, jocular but not amusing, he registered his contempt for regulations by player poker in the galley with the crew, so embarrassing some of the twenty-year men. He would chivvy the black stewards as though the Civil War had never happened. Ashore, he affected great saltiness with a rolling gait and his cap on the back of his head. He was the single officer I met who did go to the whores, then boasted about it to the rest of us.

My plan to escape Christiansen was to qualify for a command of my own. The PCs as well as the SC class were coming out of the shipyards fast, and commanders for them had to be found. As gunnery officer in Winters's ship, I set out to learn all I could about gunnery, and consciously to study every aspect of command. Midshipman training in theory proved an unsteady base for real guns in a real ship. We had no radar and no kind of electronic aid for laying the 3 inch 50; we trained and pointed the gun much as gunners had done since the eighteenth century, by guess, by god, and by adjusting over and under shots until we were on target. Daley, gunner's mate first class with a dozen years in the Navy, was my instructor, and a good one. I could make an ass of myself with stupid questions, and with tact and patience he would put me right. Winters gave me permission to drill the gun crews, dry, three or four times a week, and once or twice a week, when we were not in convoy, we fired live ammunition at a barrel a mile or so distant from the ship. Depth charges, also my responsibility, posed other dilemmas. At 300 pounds, each can (argot for depth charge) had to be hoisted from the magazine by chain fall and maneuvered

---

4. My sympathy went out to the black woman running for high office who said of her rich opponent, "His biggest struggle was out of the birth-canal."

onto the discharge racks, a bad task in a sea, dangerous to the handlers and not an easy drill.

Driscoll, the best man on the depth charge detail, was memorable. He had come out of the southern Illinois coal fields and had known bad times. The hungry years had not affected his physique or his spirit, and I was glad to have him work for me. Seasick at first, he soon got over that, but it took him time to find his ease in shipboard life. Denver, the boatswain said, "He ain't dumb. He's jest green. About the greenest I ever see in the Navy."

Driscoll had been amazed and delighted at the combined noise of the 3 inch 50 and the AA guns in drills. When we made our first honest-to-god attack on a U-boat off Puerto Rico, we released five cans from the racks and fired the port and starboard K-guns on our first run. The unearthly racket was always startling and the great, green pillars of water hard to credit, but in that first attack, Driscoll turned to the crew on the racks to say, "Now look at that. Juust look at that." In four months or so, even Denver had to admit that Driscoll was one of the most reliable men aboard. At one point I could not find my pipe with a swiveling cover, which allowed me to smoke on watch at night despite our blackout. One day Denver appeared with the pipe, beautifully decorated with elaborate knot-work. "Driscoll did it, sir, but he ast me to give it to you for your birthday." An anniversary I had totally forgotten.

Reliable at sea, Driscoll ashore turned into a menace, a drunken bar-fighter and profligate spender of hard-earned pay. After a brutal night, the Shore Patrol would carry him aboard, bleeding and happy, for trial at Captain's Mast. The master-at-arms (Denver) would read out the charges, and Winters would say, "So, Driscoll. We meet again. Do you enjoy making a mess of yourself?"

"Yes sir, captain. I guess I sure do."

"Well try to restrain your joy in the future. Dismissed."

Coldly but unobtrusively as possible, I continued to observe what I thought was good and what not so good in Winters's command of the ship. Despite Hutton's indignation, Winters encouraged me to take sun and star sights and to keep a plot for practice in celestial navigation. I avoided Christiansen and communications, but I read up on damage control and tried in vain to understand the workings of the diesel engines. Winters, however, was my primary if unconscious instructor in the science and art of commanding a small naval vessel.

He was at his best when an action loomed: at high alert, with one-half the crew in attack stations, and at general quarters, when an attack was imminent and the entire crew mobilized. Such times were comparatively infrequent, but when we were in convoy, the possibility first of the explosion, then the smoke and turmoil of a merchant ship torpedoed always nibbled at the edge of a watch officer's consciousness. In our first convoys, before the lookouts had become seasoned and before the sonar operators had learned to distinguish schools of fish, dolphins, or whales from submarines, false alarms, always at night it appeared, were frequent and exhausting. It took a good deal of seasoning to realize that a dolphin heading for the ship at night with a phosphorescent trail was not a torpedo. In our first all-too successful depth charge attack, we found that we had demolished not a submarine but a whale. Winters was patient with our errors. He would sit near the sonar screen for hours, working with the operators to discriminate various kinds of echo-response. Even turbulence in the sea would produce a mushy sort of echo, unnerving to a nineteen-year-old just out of Sound School and feeling half seasick.

At general quarters, Winters would arrive on the flying bridge to receive readiness reports, to hear the watch officer's account of what had been happening, and to assess the situation, often seeming already to have a plan in mind. Hutton would con the ship as Winters would go down to the bridge proper adjacent to the sonar screen to determine whether or not the contact justified a depth charge run. He was textbook calm throughout, no matter what confusion existed: the convoy commander in a merchant ship would signal by whistle blasts a turn away from our point of attack, creating a question of where with respect to the convoy's position the escorts belonged. Hutton would issue contrasting orders, then correct himself, further confusing matters. Messages would go to the signalmen to be relayed if we were the senior escort ship. If we were not senior, orders would come by signal flags or blinker from the senior, usually a destroyer. Destroyer commanders were prone to calling off Pcs from a contact to take over further attack and so to garner resulting credit, if any. The fact that we were more maneuverable than destroyers and better able to mount successive, rapid attacks therefore was ignored. Such procedures increased the always subterranean resentment between Annapolis men and the reserves. It had to be humiliating for Winters, himself an Annapolis man, to be ordered away from a positive sonar contact and to drop astern of the convoy to pick up survivors, but he never let resentment show.

We learned how difficult it is to kill a submarine. Sonar could give reasonably accurate bearings and distances, but it would have taken godlike skill for the sonar operator to know whether the boat had gone deep, stopped—a frequent and effective tactic—or had turned away from the immediate vicinity of our depth charge patterns. British experience extending back to 1940 had shown that often an escort would have to prolong its search and attack for eight or more hours, and even then come up dry more often than not. Our tactics, together with the scarcity of escorts before 1943, forbade the luxury of a prolonged hunt. Frustration was the order of those days.

Long after the war, people would ask if I felt no compassion for the crews in U-boats we were trying to destroy. Certainly not at the time. I can recall only one occasion on which I thought immediately of the human beings we were attacking. Not long after I took over my second command, a PC, we were proceeding independently at night off the coast of Barbados, when a lookout reported a suspicious vessel on or near the shoreline. I had been asleep in my quarters, but hurrying up to the bridge, I took the watch officer's report and ordered the helmsman to close on the shore some three miles distant; the night was clear but lit only by the stars, sufficient to confirm, as we closed, a definite outline that I, too, thought it was likely to be a submarine. We sent a demand for recognition signals, twice, and receiving none, put up a star-shell, which definitely convinced us that the vessel was a submarine, probably refueling from a clandestine source in uninhabited country. I ordered the gunners to load with armor-piercing ammunition and told the gunnery officer to commence firing. We put in two shells before the submarine submerged. We hunted her for three hours but got no sonar contact; she had clearly escaped, but with what harm? We knew that one shell at least had hit, and *miserere, miserere* came into my mind—Good Friday thoughts.

To my great satisfaction, Winters recommended me for a command after six months in his ship. I soon got orders to a new SC, even smaller than the PC at 110 feet, wooden rather than steel, and after another six months I was ordered to command of a PC. With the exception of the Barbados incident, none of us had time for compassion; we were too busy with the duties in hand. We looked on our kind of warfare as a series of technical obstructions which we had either to climb over or to obliterate, while the usual uncertainty of success filtered any urge to crow. When we were ordered to the Pacific early in 1943, however, I found the men's attitude toward the Japanese was different from their thoughts, or absence of thoughts, about the German U-boat men. When operating in the North and South Atlantic and in the Caribbean, we had had little or no news of the war in Africa or of the German advances in the Soviet Union, and none whatsoever of the concentration camps and associated outrages. In the Pacific, the Guadalcanal operation was vivid in every mind, as was Corregidor. Our own vulnerability there was not so much from Japanese submarines as from aircraft. The Japanese, fanatical and suicidal, became each man's personal enemy. Unquestionably a large vein of racial antipathy ("little yellow bastards") influenced our attitudes, quite apart from the fact that the Japanese were indoctrinated never to surrender and did not expect Caucasians to surrender.

In all theaters, we were at sea virtually all the time. In the Caribbean we would put into port: in Trinidad, Cuba, Puerto Rico, Curaçao for brief periods, a few hours, in which to fuel and provision ship, take on ammunition, collect our mail, if any, attend the next convoy-conference, then put to sea again. Life aboard an SC or a PC was physically brutal. I was astonished to read in a so-called history of antisubmarine warfare that our ships "were useful as training vessels or for convoy escort in relatively calm waters, such as the Gulf of Mexico where no enemy aircraft were present."[5] A pity the author had not been aboard my SC as we patrolled the starboard bow of a twenty-ship convoy for four days through a hurricane, or aboard one of the SCs or PCs under air attack off Guadalcanal or Iwo Jima. In those ships, any man who forgot to hang on to something firm against the motion of the ship in even a moderate sea risked maiming himself. In my bunk after a watch or prolonged nights on the bridge as ship commander, in desperation I would sometimes wedge an arm against the bulkhead, fall into fitful sleep, and wake up with a large friction bruise. Meals were chancy, and in heavy seas we existed on cheese or spam sandwiches on weevily bread and cups of rancid-tasting Navy coffee. The PC was designed to roll to 60 degrees without capsizing, and sometimes would roll all of that. Men would be flung from their bunks, work on a chart suspended while you hung on, ship's maintenance

---

5.   Blair, *Hitler's U-Boat War*, II, caption following p. 608.

was impossible, and the engine room gang would suffer tortures. We became accustomed to the uproar of the diesels and the vibration of the screws, but not to the stink of diesel exhaust when we were headed down-wind. We tried to pretend otherwise, to one another and to ourselves, but the underlying strain owing to responsibility combined with physical constraints racked the nerves as time went endlessly on. Constantly in the presence of others, we encountered the paradoxical solitude resulting from life passed among people whom you might or might not admire, with whom you probably had little genuinely in common except hour to hour experience, and people whom you probably would never see again if the war ever ended and we survived it. It was no accident that ship commanders, particularly in destroyers, were prone to breakdown.

I note such matters to emphasize that in addition to our warlike duties, routine life at sea also made, if not for breakdown, at best for the brutalization of normal, peacetime sensibilities. Although as fleet auxiliaries we were not in the forefront of any grand naval battle, our intermittent and intense episodes of naval combat, or the always imminent threat from under or above the sea, the vulnerability of the 3/8 inch steel hull, were always there in one's subconscious. We were brutalized by the tolling of the arid hours, days, months, year of the war at sea. The very expanse of the oceans made it seem sometimes as though the war would not end until we had churned through every drop of the Pacific. In the long periods of convoy duty in the Pacific over endless distances without immediate, apparent danger of action, our ability to exist without frayed nerves from the proximity and predictability of others was tested to the edge of madness. In one instance, a seaman transferred to my ship after having survived the sinking of his cruiser off Guadalcanal did go mad. We had to pry him out of the galley, where he was threatening the cooks with a .45, and transfer him at sea to a destroyer, which had a doctor aboard. We rated only a pharmacist's mate.

After the invasion of Kwajalein, my ship operated for four months between Kwajalein and the 180th meridian. We would escort three or four merchant ships in ballast on their way back to the United States to that arbitrary point on the chart, east of which they were considered safe from submarine or air attack. We would then proceed independently back to Kwajalein to repeat the voyage. I personally minded less than most of the others. The business of navigating and running the ship occupied me, and I learned to find the sea and the theatrical Pacific skies, hypnotic and fascinating by day and night. One or two others aboard shared my pleasure in the elements, but no more.

Ships' officers had one duty that I found humiliating: to censor the enlisted men's outgoing mail, a duty I was happy to delegate when I had my own command. Leese, the exec in my second command, was a decent man, unusually ascetic, and among a pack of would-be rakehells, puritanical. A former accountant, he took his position more seriously than it warranted. He positively enjoyed censoring the crew's letters, a reaction I could neither understand nor admire. At one juncture on the 180th meridian run, he came to me one say saying, "Captain, something funny is going on."

"What are you talking about?"

"Well," long pause, "some of the men are writing to their women in code. I'm pretty sure of that."

"Unless you're completely sure, forget it."

Any mention of our whereabouts or of convoy movements was of course forbidden, but I had confidence in the crew's knowledge that their own safety lay in obeying the stricture. The mystery was solved when we picked up a bag of ship's mail at the end of our run. We were at anchor in Kwajalein Atoll; late in a peaceful afternoon, the men were reading their mail. I had read my own and was smoking my pipe and chatting with Max, the gunnery officer. We were leaning on the railing of the flying bridge, and below us, not far off, half a dozen sailors were engrossed in some sort of game. Without intending to overhear them, Max and I soon figured out what they were up to. Their talk had to do with color, length, tactile quality: they were pretend-quarreling about the relative merits of the pubic hairs their women had been instructed to include in their letters, in language that Leese had inferred to be code.

Over fried spam that evening in the wardroom, Max and I described the drama. Leese was outraged; he wanted those men to be punished. My own sensibility by then was such that I told Leese the men deserved not punishment but a medal.

"How are we to punish anyone out here? A fine? They have nothing to spend money on anyway. Extra duty? Plenty of that already. Stuff them down the lazarette? They'd suffocate. Anyway, what's the charge? I don't remember anything in Naval Regulations against men receiving pubic hair in the mail. Do you?"

Devoted of the letter of Naval law, Leese was all the more uncertain that I was too lenient, a difference between us never to be resolved.

Fifty and more years after the end of it all, a farrago of incident relating to those war years remains in the mind, and still, on occasion, in dreams. I think of Denver, boatswain's mate in Winters's ship, who took over the wheel during one of my mid-watches. The sea was rough, our zig-zag pattern complex, and I was happy to have an experienced man on the helm. A tall, gangling fellow, he had put in many years in the Navy and looked forward to peace and his pension. It was Denver who said of one of the seamen, "He's so dumb he has to look in his hat when you ask him his name." After an hour of silence except for standard responses to commands, "Sir," he asked me, "are you in love with your wife?"

His question was astonishing, for it broke a rigid code of manners relating to distance between men and officers, and my first impulse was to say he was impertinent. My marriage was none of his business, but then I knew it would be cruel to ignore the sincerity in his voice. "Yes, of course. I wouldn't have married her if I hadn't been in love with her." That was all; my answer seemed to startle him, and I could only wonder why, and I still do as I consider a long list of motives, none ever to be clear because of that rigid code, now become quaint, outdated.

Rescuing survivors of ships torpedoed in the Caribbean: the images remain vivid. When a tanker went up in a black cloud under a half-moon sky, only two men as far as we could make out were able to swim through a fiery sea to our cargo net. In charge on the fantail, I directed settings on the reloaded depth charge racks, and with the pharmacist's mate gave the two survivors ampoules of morphine. Usually one ampoule would be effective promptly, but not that time. We gave them more morphine, to no visible effect. They had bad burns, and from their vomiting and choking they must have swallowed burning fuel. They remained conscious, all too conscious, and begged us to shoot them. Just then we were ordered to make a sweep on the starboard quarter of the convoy, and in perhaps half an hour one sufferer died, then the other. I had seen dead men before. First my grandfather, when I was thirteen. He was laid out in a coffin and made up with powder and lipstick like a woman; I hardly recognized him. Then Eddy, the dishwasher in a restaurant I worked in when I was in high school. I came in early one Sunday morning in winter to open up and found Eddy stiff and stinking on his sleeping—pallet in the back pantry. A gone drunk, he had downed canned heat, which was mostly wood alcohol. Those things flashed through my mind as I checked the 40 mm crew. We were still rounding up merchant ships that had made a wrong turn, the sea was running too high even had it been possible to transfer the corpses, and too dangerous, impossible, in submarine country. The bodies rolled to the ship's motion, but no mistaking their deadness. We had no place to stow corpses, we were desperately busy in that dark night, and there was nothing for it but to bury the two poor devils at sea as decently as our haste allowed.

In the Pacific a year later, my ship was ordered to escort an ammunition ship at top speed to the fleet off Tarawa. The invasion, which cold military history pronounced a success, certainly did not look it, nor did the 997 dead and 2,000 wounded bear witness to such a conclusion. Our intelligence was criminally stupid for having confused the times of high and low tide at Tarawa, hence the Marines went in at high tide and many were shot in the water. When we arrived, the island was technically secure, but still a bloated body of a Marine surged here and there in a slight surf. I went ashore for orders; tripping on something in the sand, I saw it was a human arm. The Seabees were resurfacing the bombed airstrip, and small arms fire sounded sporadically from the mopping-up still in progress.

The air-raid siren howled, and a Marine directing traffic hurried me into a Japanese bunker, eighteen feet down and untouched by the pre-invasion naval and air bombardment. In the semi-dark bunker, I made out six Japanese, or Korean, prisoners, squatting naked but for a loin cloth, guarded by two Marine privates. I protested automatically when, for no reason, one Marine jabbed at a prisoner with his bayonet. The Marine turned on me and raged, "Sailor, you go sail your fucking boat and leave us the hell alone." If I had been wearing a sidearm I'd have been tempted to use it, but the all-clear sounded and the Marines herded the prisoners up the tunnel. I had a good idea of what those prisoners' fate would be, but I did not linger long enough to prove my hunch correct.

On our next trip to Tarawa I heard that the admiral commanding had diverted some of the Seabees from reconstruction to the creation of a tennis court. That looked to be gospel when a staff officer came aboard to ask if we had any tennis players. We had. I played an average game, but a new arrival aboard, Lt. (j.g.) Farragut, in civilian life had been not only a racing car driver but also a champion tennis player. Informed of that, the staff man told us, grammatically, "It would be better if the Admiral were to win." The admiral and his doubles partner did not win. So in memory the awful and trivial combine into a ludicrous patchwork.

Other alarums and many, many excursions crowd the stirred memory or lie partially dormant in a pair of surviving notebooks: running off Eniwetok at night, being taken for a submarine by an American Liberator who did not recognize our recognition signals and taking a bomb uncomfortably close to the ship. Or my "attack" on a Japanese resupply vessel off one of their islands which had been beached and abandoned; the badly cut up company of Marines we transported from one island to another in that area: men wanting only water and sleep, who made me thank the gods for not having become a Marine.

The U-boat bunkers at Lorient, with the *Île de Ré* just across the water, performed the service, or disservice, of reviving all too vividly the years from 1941–1945. At the longed-for end of it, the war seemed not to end dramatically as wars are supposed to end, but slowly to deflate. After a year in various naval hospitals, I could only reflect again that each year of the unending war had consumed another chunk of our precious youth. Those years were our time of wild oats without oats or time, our *vie de bohéme* with neither life nor bohemians; we had sailed everywhere but we hadn't been anywhere, and there was nothing to show for it but churned sea-water and morose thanksgiving that Hiroshima and Nagasaki had saved us from the invasion of Japan. I think that many of us had a sort of schizophrenia about the war. We were spared the convictions of many post-World War I men that it had been a pointless slaughter, leading only to the farce of disarmament and the rise of German Nazism, Italian and Soviet fascism. We were also spared the scorn that men back from Vietnam on the sunny side of a body bag experienced. We could and did believe that if such a thing as a just war exists, ours had been that war. I heard no serving man debate the justice of the war, nor was there much jingoism. Only one acquaintance, an intense fellow from Alabama, quoted to me, "My country, right or wrong, my country." I was to learn that he died for his country in a submarine that never returned to base. I was simply resigned to the war; I could not love it, but I would not have missed it. Aged twenty-nine when I was discharged, I was oppressed and depressed by civilian life. Naval service, however, enabled me to return to study in a good university and so to qualify for an uneven but bearable postwar existence. More than any other factor, the war marked me for life. Embarking on civilian life, I felt a shocking wrench, but I believed that nothing in civilian life could ever again threaten me or be anything but easy compared with the war. I was wrong, to be sure, for at twenty-nine I was not able to credit what "normal," alleged peace could do to us, to all of us.

As our miserable century gibbers to a close, I am alarmed that the young get their history of my increasingly popular war from films purporting to record truths about the combatants and about combat. They are given to believe that the war was fought almost exclusively by the U.S. Army and Corps of Marines, with the British, the Canadians, the Free French, and the Soviets somewhere off in the wings. That Hollywoodization of the war led one critic to write of the money-maker, *Saving Private Ryan*, that a relative of his, a veteran of D-Day, spoke of comrades falling only on the periphery of vision, "'but you've got your own life to look out for,—you're not clocking every artery, every splintered skull.'" "But Hollywood is in the simplification business: in Spielberg's so-called 'realistic' D-Day sequence...we see nothing but one individual death after another, in detail. Every action is ignoble: when our boys eventually reach the enemy bunker and set it afire, the Germans come scrambling out, screaming in agony, and the American shouts to his men, '"Don't fire! Let them burn!"' This isn't reality, it's fashion."[6]

So multifarious a war resists treatment in film, and so far, in fiction. War films are insulting to the many good and not-so good men who did not return from it, and to those who returned to a long half-life in hospitals. It is equally insulting to offer the young pseudo-realism and "fashion" as an easy way around the demanding study of written history, in which no easy answers to hard questions are served up.

That war is exciting and to many combatants, a form of escape, while at the same time those combatants know that it is the negation of moral value and of life itself, forms a paradox that we can neither resolve nor live with. The dialectical opposite of war, pacifism, however admirable in its stance, still strikes me as blind to the realities of

---

6. Mark Steyn, "The Entertainment State," *The New Criterion* (xvii, no.1, September 1998) 25–26.

human and political stupidity. War poses one of the many questions to which no one has devised an answer: cold comfort, but cold comfort is still comfort of a sort, and, sadly, the best we have devised.

Coda:
Closet Space

Those who survive into old age in our society find themselves skirmishing with the mortality tables, for the future lies well astern. They struggle with memory, that curse and comfort, while death, daily, is on the mind, and any effort to ignore it constitutes a foolish evasion and betrayal of the integral self. The marks of our skirmish lie on our faces raddled by wrinkles and in our rheumatic groans. The young, for whom death has no reality, fear us: the civilized among them show us exaggerated courtesy; the semi-civilized ignore us; the barbarians see us as fair game for assault. We are a statistical embarrassment, since medicine, where available, has endowed us with additional years to burden the politician and to distort many a social tale about family solidarity. Much of the time the old are simply invisible. Out on the streets the young do not see an individual with a history, a present and a future; they see An Old Woman or An Old Man, lacking in specific traits, like Lowry's matchstick people.

That is not all to the bad, for knowledge of one's invisibility may liberate the old from certain social inhibitions. They tend to speak their minds where in the past they would have bitten their tongues. They address strangers without inner impediment. The knowledge of death, even if never articulated, frees the old from the constraints of group or class. Old age is rarely serene: the seven deadly sins are never far off. Pride rages on, even after a fall; lechery still lurks. I know an eminent man in his mid-eighties who paws young women at parties and recounts to each new acquaintance the number and occasions of his sexual triumphs. Envy is ever-present; anger roars up, followed by shame; covetousness knows no age, nor does gluttony, while sloth is the particular curse of the aged. They have so many reasons not to act, they tell themselves, as they slump back on the sofa.

163

In old age, surprises may abound. Small pleasures become bigger, and new, unexpected pleasures arise. I was seventy-five before I discovered the pleasure of feeding the song birds outside the dining-room window, or really seeing the winter jasmine on our stone wall in glum February. Despite my words about the young, I have learned the satisfaction to be had in the movement from new acquaintance to genuine friendship with people young enough to be my children. Frances Partridge, at age 101 and still writing, remarked, "What I most dread is that life should slip by unnoticed, like a scene half-glimpsed from a railway carriage window." Yes, and yes. One has lost the spontaneity of corybantic youth, but the attempt to come to terms with one's convictions and prejudices can deliver a sense of inner ease.

In our country, for one example, death is a dirty word, perhaps the only dirty word left in our language. The man's black suit and the widow's weeds, sartorial suttee, haven't been seen for decades. The wake is regarded as drunken paganism (and may well be).The corpse is hastily reduced to ashes or stuffed in the ground to a gathering of mourners who, if technically Christian, have long forgotten the words to the prayers. Biographers write of their subjects as "facing up to the terrors of mortality." Why should this be? I ask myself.

An answer, like all such answers to large moral questions, is both blindingly obvious and maddeningly elusive. It is obvious that people should prefer life to death, but with only the tatters of religion extant, with the sense of the sacred, which is equivalent to the Platonic Good, supplanted by the religion of youth and facial collagen for the wrinkled, death becomes the dirty meaning assigned to it. What I find elusive is wrapped in my prejudice that our rationality is really all we have, however unreliable and rare it may be. At the same time, if you don't believe in God, that backstop, you had better believe in your own ideas. I must repeat that religion, or the parody of religion that now flourishes, teaches many of us neither how to live nor how to die. I find it arrogant to believe that we are special in nature, chosen. How can we be? for our death is as natural as our birth and breathing in the time between that nature grants us. It is therefore sentimental and absurd to fear death. Mysticism of any stripe defies such a conclusion, but for a fair number of us, mysticism, not death, is the fearful enemy.

Much of this is summed up in the anecdote of the woman whose husband had recently died. When a neighbor asked how she was getting along after her loss, she answered, "Of course I miss him very much, but it is lovely to have the closet space."

Heartless perhaps, pragmatic indeed, resistant to the tragic view of life, but neither mystical nor sentimental, and reassuringly honest. Must we ask for more?